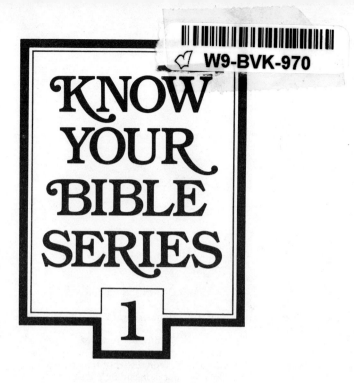

KNOW YOUR BIBLE SERIES

1

INTRODUCTION TO YOUR BIBLE

ROY L. SMITH

ABINGDON PRESS
NASHVILLE

Introduction to Your Bible

Revised Edition

Copyright 1943, 1955. Copyright renewal © 1970 by Mrs. Mabel Conley Smith.

No. 209129

Printed in U.S.A.

INTRODUCTION

During recent years we have been using the scientific method in studying the Bible, and this has resulted in a vast increase in our knowledge and understanding of the Christian scriptures. Unfortunately much of this new information has been shut up inside the schools and has not been utilized by the plain people who go to their Bible for inspiration and help. As a result many cults and sects have fattened upon the fact that lay people in large numbers remain ignorant of the background of their Bible and the conditions under which it came to its present completion.

There is a very great reverence for the Bible, particularly among Christian people; but reverence that remains ignorant is sometimes as dangerous to the cause of good religion as outright antagonism. It is highly important that the Church shall give its people adequate and reliable information concerning the book which is central in their faith.

Great truths of the Bible wait to serve us. From no other source have we drawn such treasures as from the Bible, and its store remains inexhaustible. As old as creation, and as modern as this morning's sunrise, "the truth and the way" await us on the pages of this holy book.

This course of lessons has been prepared for laypeople, that they may have the benefit of the highly valuable study and research which has been made in their behalf. The author does not pretend to be an investigator in the field. He is only a reporter who has studied the findings of the scholars, and then attempts to translate them into the language of the layman.

In order that he might be sure he was reporting the scholars correctly, the author has submitted the manuscript to a board of editors, each one of whom is a specialist in his field. They have read it carefully, correcting, clarifying, and checking it. In some instances they have submitted it to other scholars for additional inspection. Though none of them can be held responsible for specific statements, it may be said that they are in general agreement as to the accuracy of the reporting.

Delicate questions of great interest to scholars, and which are the occasion of considerable debate without final settlement, have been ignored for the most part in the belief that the ordinary layperson is not particularly interested. Our concern is in the devotional and inspirational values of the Scriptures.

The catechism style of presentation has been chosen because of the ease with which the student can move from one problem to another. A plain and humble Christian can sit down with these studies and, with no other aid than the Bible, get a comprehensive view of the whole field of the Scriptures. It is not even necessary to be a member of any Bible class to follow the course through, though many will find the class method of study of greater inspiration.

We are now ready to start on a great adventure—the rediscovery of the Book which has been the greatest single influence on history of any piece of literature ever produced. It will be a thrilling experience for all valiant and honest souls who really seek the truth. But it will be necessary for each student to come to the Bible with an open mind. Some old misconceptions may have to be dismissed. At times it may be necessary to trust the author, for the limitations of space prevent him from presenting all the evidence in some cases. But it is at this point that the approval of the editorial board has special value. Their reputation for Christian sincerity and integrity is a guarantee that the student is not being led astray. Those who will set out with determination and reverence will come through to the end of the course with a new Bible—one that will thrill the imagination and build up within their lives a triumphant faith.

Roy L. Smith

How Your
Bible Grew Up

1 What is the Bible?

The Bible is a collection of ancient writings composed of the sacred scriptures of the Jewish and the Christian religions.

2 What is meant by a "collection of ancient writings"?

There is a sense in which the Bible can be compared to the "Harvard Classics." President Eliot of Harvard University once remarked in the course of an address that anyone could get a liberal education if he or she would read the books that could be set up on a five-foot shelf. The books would have to be chosen wisely, of course, and the reader would have to read intelligently. But the basis of a broad culture and a good education could be thus briefly presented.

An enterprising publisher thereupon asked Dr. Eliot to make a selection of those books which would, in his opinion, furnish that "liberal education," and they were soon thereafter offered to the reading public under the title "The Harvard Classics." None of the books had been written for any such shelf, and no author had written in the hope that his writing would be so honored. Each book had earned its right to be included in such a shelf long before Dr. Eliot selected it or even suggested such a shelf. The famous educator did no more than choose those which, in his judgment, measured up to the high standard he had set. In making his selection he was under the necessity of laying aside many valuable books. Perhaps another person would have included them. In the end the set sold hundreds of thousands of copies of the books which were included because the public believed in the ability of Harvard's great president to make wise choices.

In something of the same way the Bible came into existence. Many books had been produced, some of which were very valuable. Then there came a time when a collection was needed which the people could trust, and men in whom the Jews had great confidence because of their piety and learning chose those books which are to be found in the Old Testament; other men in whom the Christians had confidence selected those books to be found in the New Testament.

As we proceed further with this study, we will discover that those who selected the books to be included were not always in strict agreement. In fact, in a few cases, there was for a time at least sharp difference of opinion. But in the end there has been more or less general agreement inside the great body of believers.

3 What is meant by "books"?

Exactly what the word means. The Bible is not actually one book, but a collection of books. It might be called a library. Long before anyone assembled them in one volume the various books circulated independently of each other, and most of them enjoyed a wide reading long before they were accorded a place in the collection of accepted scriptures.

4 Who wrote the Bible?

Many people, writing at different places and at different times for different reasons. The names of some of the authors are well known, while the names of those who authored other books have been lost and will probably never be known. As a whole, however, it can be said that the Bible was written by Hebrews, although at least two books (Luke and Acts) are believed to have been written by a young Greek physician. Some few fragments (in Psalms and Proverbs) seem to have been written originally by unknown Egyptian authors, for they were widely circulated in Egypt before they appeared in the Bible. The ancient Hebrews, sensing their religious worth, appropriated them and included them in their own literature.

5 Where was the Bible written?

In general it can be said that the Old Testament was written in Palestine, but much of the New Testament was written outside the Holy Land. The letters of Paul, for example, were written from several cities in which the Great Apostle was engaged in missionary work in Europe and Asia, some of them being penned while he was in prison in Rome.

6 For what purpose was the Bible written?

To answer this question satisfactorily we must answer for

each book. Some were written for political, some for philo-sophic, some for historical, and some for religious reasons. Broadly speaking, all were included because of the belief that each would make some contribution to religious life.

7 When was the Bible written?

Some brief poetical fragments quoted in the Old Testament historical books may have been composed as early as the thirteenth century before Christ. Much of the vivid story of Absalom's revolt against his father, King David, as it is told in Second Samuel must have been written by an eyewitness, who would have been writing in the tenth century. The first book to be set down in approximately its present form is Amos, dating from the eighth century. At the other end the last of the New Testament books, Second Peter, may have been composed as late as A.D. 150. Thus it can be said that the writing of the Bible stretched out over a period of fifteen centuries. And in fact some portion of the Bible can be traced to each of those centuries.

8 What is the Old Testament?

The word "testament" means "covenant" or "agreement." When the Hebrews came out of Egypt under Moses' leadership, they entered into a solemn agreement (it could almost be called a contract) with Jehovah by which they bound themselves to serve him (Exodus 19 through Numbers 10), and Jehovah was to guard and guide them. This "covenant" became the foundation of all their national philosophy and religious thought. The Old Testament can be called the record of the Hebrew people as they lived under this agreement.

9 What is the New Testament?

With the rise of the Christian faith the Christians declared that a new covenant had been offered people in the death and resurrection of Jesus. By this they meant that all people might become members of the "chosen people" if they were willing to believe in Jesus as the revelation of God, and in his death upon the cross as the assurance of God's willingness to forgive their sins. It was no longer necessary for one to become a member of the Jewish race in order to share in God's grace and favor. One might become one of the "chosen" by entering into a spiritual fellowship with Jesus Christ. This new covenant is the theme of the New Testament.

10 What is the difference between the two Testaments?

Aside from the difference in their themes the two Testaments are alike in many respects. Each represents a collection of books; each represents a series of choices made by godly people acting on deeply religious motives; each represents a variety of viewpoints; the books in both collections circulated widely and independently through many years prior to the time they appeared in their respective Testaments; they came to be called scripture by the slow process of popular acceptance followed after many years by some form of official sanction.

On the other hand, there are marked differences between them. The older is a record of a nation, and the newer is the record of a religious movement. The Old Testament tells the story of many national heroes; the New Testament came into existence as the result of the life and teachings of a single personality. The Old Testament was assembled for the spiritual guidance of the Jewish people; the New Testament was assembled for the religious nurture of all. Jews accept the Old Testament as their inspired scripture; Christians accept both Testaments as containing the word of God.

11 What is meant by scripture?

The dictionary defines "scripture" as being any sacred writing. The Hindu religion has a very extensive sacred literature, of which the most influential work today is the Bhagavad-Gita; Moslems have the Koran; Confucians turn to the Five Classics and some supplementary materials; Buddhists turn to the Tripitaka. All these are highly revered by those who accept them as scripture, but to the Christian the Bible is accorded a reverence that is just a little different. It is to them the book of final spiritual authority in which they read the word of God to them.

12 What kind of literature does the Bible contain?

History (Acts), hymns (Psalms), legal codes (Deuteronomy), personal letters (Philemon), fiction (Esther), love lyrics (Song of Solomon), sermons (James), epigrams (Proverbs), official

8

records (Kings), personal memoirs (Ezra and Nehemiah), propaganda (Ruth), pageantry (Nahum), and drama (Job). This does not exhaust the list, but it suggests the variety.

13 What does all this mean?

It means that each type of material must be interpreted according to the principles which apply in such cases. Poetry, for example, is not to be read as one would read simple history. Fiction employs its own method for presenting truth. Personal letters come to have meaning when we know to whom and by whom they were written.

14 Does this make the Bible hard to read?

Not necessarily, though it does mean that it must be read with care. It also means that the reader needs much more information, to understand some passages, than that which appears on the pages of the Bible itself.

15 Is it possible for ordinary people to read the Bible?

Certainly. A very great part of the Bible is so plainly written, and its meaning is so evident, that even a child can understand it. In other instances, however, plain people will find obscure passages cleared up for them by the facts which are brought to light by the scholars who have made it their lifework to find them.

16 Are the different types of literature plainly marked?

In some books—such as Acts, Kings, Chronicles—the reader recognizes the material as being historical. But in the case of drama, fiction, and poetry the average individual may have some difficulty. Hebrew poetry, for example, does not rhyme when translated into English, nor is it always easy to bring the rhythm over from one language into another. The translators are therefore under the necessity of doing something to identify the original literary form in which it was written. It is one of the defects of the King James Version of the Bible that it makes no effort to identify poetry. It is one of the advantages of the Revised Standard Version that it makes poetry perfectly plain.

17   Does it make any great difference?

It can make a very great deal of difference. If an Old Testament book was written as fiction and if it was read as such by its original readers, they got one idea from it. If its modern readers read it as sober history, they may get an entirely different idea from it—one that the author never intended they should get. The book of Jonah, in the Old Testament, is an excellent illustration. It is a book *about* a prophet, and not one *by* a prophet. It was written originally in the hope that it might convince the Jews of their missionary responsibilities for the non-Jewish world. But when it is read as sober history, the interest centers in the fish episode, and the spiritual lesson originally intended is lost.

18   Is it not strange that there should be fiction in the Bible?

It should not seem so, for fiction is a perfectly legitimate method for presenting truth. Lew Wallace's epic story *Ben Hur* is a devout book which undertakes to present a great spiritual truth in story form. No one would think of discrediting it because it is not factual history. Jesus presented some of his most important ideas in story form, and the people recognized them for exactly what they were (Mark 4:2) and profited by them. In this he did exactly what many other rabbis of his time did—he preached in parables. The people had learned to listen to truth taught by that method. No one questions the validity of the things Jesus said because of the form in which he presented his ideas, nor because he invented stories for the purpose of making his points. The difficulty arises, perhaps, from the fact that we misunderstand "fiction" to mean something that is not true, and it cannot be used in that sense in speaking of the fiction of the Bible. The word is the name applied to a form of literary expression.

19   With what subjects does the Old Testament deal?

With almost every subject having an interest for serious-minded readers—politics, economics, social ethics, international affairs, dreams, love, sex, social legislation, history, sanitation, race problems, peace diplomacy, intrigue, riddles, military strategy, and many other things.

20 In what language was the Bible written?

The Old Testament was written in Hebrew, with the exception of some brief portions which were written in Aramaic (Daniel 2:4—7:28); Ezra 4:8—6:18; 7:12-26; Jeremiah 10:11). The New Testament was written in Greek, although it contains some Aramaic phrases. Some few scholars believe the four Gospels were written in Aramaic originally, and translated into Greek, but this theory has not been proved and is not widely accepted.

21 What was Aramaic?

It was Jesus' mother tongue, the common speech of the Jews who lived in Palestine during his time. It was a language close of kin to Hebrew but sufficiently different that if one had been reared to speak it he would find it very difficult, if not impossible, to understand Hebrew. Following the destruction of the Temple in 586 B.C. and the exile of the Hebrew people in Babylonia, the use of their ancestral tongue declined. Children born in the exile quite naturally learned to speak the language of the land of their birth. Because of the pressure Persia exerted on her dependencies (538-331 B.C.) there was a tendency for Aramaic to become the common language of all the East Mediterranean area. The wretched remnant left behind in Judea when the exiles were carried off so far adopted the Aramaic that Nehemiah complained bitterly when he returned to rebuild Jerusalem in 445 B.C., that they spake "half in the speech of Ashdod, and could not speak in the Jews' language" (13:24). Long before the birth of Jesus the use of Hebrew, except in learned and classical circles, had practically ceased.

22 Where did the Greek come in?

The first Christians were Jews and, of course, spoke Aramaic as Jesus did. Within the space of less than one hundred years, however, the Christian movement had gone over into the Gentile world where Greek was spoken, and it was among the Gentile Christians that the New Testament writings came into existence. As a consequence the earliest New Testament manuscripts were in Greek with only an occasional Aramaic expression included.

11

23 How did the Bible get into English?

At least some Christian missionary work was done in England in the third century, but the significant evangelization of the British Isles began in A.D. 597, when Pope Gregory sent a group of missionaries to convert the land. Relatively few of the Britons could read, for they were a primitive people, and the faith had to be propagated by means of sermons, songs, and oral recitals of the great Christian story. Some small portions of the Scripture were set down in written form by occasional individuals and a few comments (very few) on particular passages were published. But there was a widespread prejudice against all such activity, it being believed that the Scriptures were profaned if they fell into the hands of people as uncouth as the English were esteemed to be at that time. As English learning developed, however, this prejudice was attacked and a demand began to be heard that the Bible be made accessible to the people.

24 Who made this demand?

They were religious men, of course, inside the church. They were also devout men with a sense of mission who believed that the benefits of Christianity should be made available to the plain people by every possible means.

25 When was something done about it?

During the fourteenth century an eloquent Oxford University scholar named John Wycliffe (1324?-1384) succeeded in translating the Scriptures from Latin into the common speech. He died a natural death; but his work aroused so much opposition on the part of other churchmen that in 1428 his bones were exhumed and burned, and the ashes were thrown into the River Swift as an indication of the disfavor in which his "crime" was held. His work survived, however, and was the only English Bible available until William Tyndale did his work in the sixteenth century.

26 What about William Tyndale?

Sometime about 1520 William Tyndale, a scholar educated at Oxford and Cambridge, came to believe that it would be "impossible to stablysh the laye people in any truth, excepte the scripture were playnly layde before their eyes in their mother tongue." He determined to make a translation of the Bible directly from the original Hebrew and Greek texts (which the invention of printing had just made available) into the common English speech of his day. To one of the bishops of the church he declared, "If God spare my lyfe, ere many yeares I wyl cause a boye that dryveth the plough shall know more of the scripture than thou doest!" He set to work, but opposition of the authorities soon forced him to leave England for Germany. Here he completed the New Testament in the summer of 1525; and printing was started, only to be interrupted by official action. The work was secretly transferred to another city and resumed, and soon New Testaments printed in the common tongue were being smuggled into England. Meanwhile Tyndale began translating the Hebrew Old Testament. But the persecution grew; and eventually he was betrayed to his enemies, seized, strangled, and burned at the stake on October 6, 1536. At that time he had finished translating only half the Old Testament. His work influenced all subsequent translations in a very profound way, however, and to him must go the honor of having done more to set the pattern for English translation than any other English scholar.

27 When was a complete English Bible printed?

During Tyndale's later years another English scholar, named Miles Coverdale, was living in Germany, having been compelled to flee England because of his Protestant convictions. He had met Tyndale some years earlier and become inspired by that great scholar's devotion to the Bible. He undertook to translate some sections of it himself. To his own work he added that of Tyndale and in 1535 published the first complete Bible to be issued in the English language.

28 Was Coverdale's Bible permitted to circulate?

By this time the leaders of the English church had come to see the value of the Bible in the language of the people. Though the change of viewpoint did not save Tyndale, it kept the authorities from stopping importation of Coverdale's Bible. In fact within a few months official orders were drawn up that every parish church must have an English Bible, and Coverdale was commissioned to revise his translation in order to supply the Bibles needed. This revision was issued in 1539 as the first English "authorized version," and came to be known as the Great Bible.

29 What is an "authorized version"?

One that is officially sponsored for use in public worship. The Great Bible was of course intended for use in the parish churches of the Established Church in England.

30 Why was it called the Great Bible?

Because it was printed in a very large size, being designed for use in the pulpits of the churches. It is interesting to know that one portion of this old translation is still used in public worship.

31 What portion is still used?

Not long after the appearance of the Great Bible the English *Book of Common Prayer* was composed for the aid of the people, and its Psalter was taken from the Great Bible. As a consequence British Anglicans, and Episcopalians in the United States, recite their responsive lessons from Coverdale's translation to this day.

32 Was this Bible widely read?

It must be remembered that reading was not the universal art of today. Many very intelligent people were able to assume great responsibilities and enjoyed considerable culture, but were not skilled in reading and writing. Because of the expense involved, and the desire to protect the Scriptures from the contaminating touch of the common people, the Great Bible was used almost entirely in the pulpits of the churches, where it was read by the priests of the church.

33 When did a household Bible appear?

In 1553 Mary Tudor, a devout Catholic, came to the throne in England and undertook to lead the nation back into the Roman fold. A considerable number of Protestants, fearful for their lives and their religious liberties, fled to Europe and congregated at Geneva, Switzerland, where they established contact with the leaders of continental Protestantism. Inspired by those great souls they undertook as a co-operative labor to translate the Scriptures into English, having the hope that it would serve the same purpose in the British Isles that Luther's translation had served among the German-speaking people. The Bible they produced was published in 1560, and came to be called the Geneva Bible. As a translation it leaned heavily upon the work already done by Tyndale and was, on the whole, a very superior piece of work. It quickly became popular for home reading.

34 Did the Geneva Bible supersede the Great Bible?

English Protestantism, quite unhappily, was divided into numerous parties, the antagonisms between them often being as deep as between Catholic and Protestant. As the Puritan movement grew following the accession of Queen Elizabeth I, it supported the Geneva Bible. The bishops of the Established Church, rather than accept the new translation's popularity, tried to compete with it by revising the Great Bible. This second authorized version appeared in 1568 and acquired the name Bishops' Bible, for obvious reasons. It did not succeed in winning people away from the Geneva Bible, which went on to be the version read by Shakespeare, John Bunyan, John Milton, Cromwell's army, and even King James himself, whose name is attached to the English Bible best known today—the King James Version.

35 What is the King James Version?

King James of England, a Protestant, and something of a biblical scholar in his own right, was approached by a group of Protestant leaders with the suggestion that a new translation of the Bible be undertaken. It was further suggested that it might have the effect of uniting Protestants and bringing an end to the sorry divisions which were the shame of the movement. In 1604 a committee of fifty "learned men" was organized and given careful instructions as to how to proceed with their work. Every precaution was to be exercised that the translation should be accurate, faithful to the Christian tradition, composed in the best English style, and free from partisan bias.

After some delays they got down to work, and the third authorized English version came from the press in 1611.

36 How was the King James Version received?

The Puritans, being well satisfied with the Geneva Bible, refused to have anything to do with it. The American reader will be interested to know that the Bible brought to the New World by the Pilgrims who settled in Massachusetts in 1620 was the Geneva Version. Among the plain people, particularly the Puritans, it had developed such great popularity as the household Bible of English Protestantism that it could not easily be displaced. For a period of many years the King James Version had to meet bitter opposition in spite of the fact that the great influence of the king and the Established Church was behind the newer version.

37 What was the objection to it?

Just as partisans had charged a hundred years earlier that Tyndale's translation "perverted" the true meaning of the Scriptures, so those opposed to the King James Version declared it presented a biased viewpoint.

38 Was this objection justified?

A part of the objection was the result of sectarian prejudice. But, it must be admitted, the translation was not entirely free from errors. Many of these were corrected following the appearance of the original edition in 1611, but the new editions also supplied some of their own as might have been expected, because of typographical errors and the like. As many as fifty editions had been published by 1640; and thereafter editions showing revisions appeared from time to time, the last and most important being that of Benjamin Blayney, published at Oxford in 1769. As a result of all these printings and revisions it must be said that no one today reads the King James Version precisely as it appeared in 1611.

Objection was raised on another score, quite aside from all question of errors in the text. There were no Sunday-school helps or other religious literature for the education of the laity in 1600, with the result that many Bibles were printed with explanatory notes in the margins. These "notes" were often partisan, or sectarian in nature, since they reflected the personal opinions of the translator or the printer. Thus, a Puritan Bible might abound in Puritan notes and explanations of the text, and an Anglican Bible might present the viewpoint of that body in many cases. The "learned men" who translated the King James Version were instructed to omit all notes, but in spite of that some 8,000 notes and 9,000 cross references did appear. While these were of no great importance as bases of controversy, they did provide the opportunity for objections—if only because desired notes were omitted.

39 Was the King James Version partisan?

Its translators strove diligently to avoid making it so. In the first place, it represented the judgment of at least fifty different scholars, each man having presented his viewpoint and having submitted it to the inspection and criticism of all the others. The final result was as nearly a unanimous opinion as could have been reached. In the second place, as has just been suggested, it was published with a minimum of notes. In view of all the facts it can probably be said that it was the least partisan of any English Bible in existence in 1611. That did not silence its critics, however, for it was compelled to battle for its place and popularity through a period of at least seventy-five years, in spite of the powerful sponsorship under which it was launched.

40 Did Roman Catholics accept the King James Version?

The agitation which has been described up to this point arose entirely inside the ranks of Protestantism. The Protestants, it must be remembered, were divided into sects and groups, each one taking its own position. In the meantime the Roman Catholic Church produced its own English version, which came to be called the Douay Bible.

41 What was the Douay Bible?

Quite unhappily, religious dissension in England resulted in sternly repressive measures by the party in power. When Roman Catholic Queen Mary sat upon the throne, the Protestants lived under various bans; then when Protestant Queen Elizabeth came to the throne, the Catholics suffered. During this latter period a group of Catholics took refuge in France, and a brilliant scholar among them named William Cardinal Allen founded an English college at Douai. These refugees recognized the disadvantages under which their coreligionists labored in England as a result of having no Bible in English. If Roman Catholic priests and teachers were to hold their own against the Protestants, they must be able to quote the Scriptures; and if this was to be done with authority, there must be a standard text available to them. It was not expected that Catholic laymen were to be furnished the Scriptures (as was the case to a considerable extent among the Protestants). Rather, it as to be a tool for the priests. The refugee scholars therefore translated the Latin Vulgate and published the New Testament in 1582, the Old Testament following in 1610. To this translation was given the name Douay or Rheims-Douay.

42 Why was this name chosen?

The name was not chosen by the translators, but it was given to the Bible by the public because the work of translating was done by the English scholars in the two cities of Rheims and Douai. The English college had removed from Douai for a short time, settling in Rheims. The actual work of translating went on in both cities.

43 How did the Douay Version differ?

It was published quite honestly and frankly to be used by the Catholic clergy in combating the English Protestants. Quite legitimately it included various marginal notes of interest to Catholics, and used words with which the Catholic priests were especially familiar. For example, in the Lord's Prayer (Matthew 6:11) it was made to read "Give us to day our super-substantial bread." Because of the fact that it was translated directly from the Latin Vulgate it often followed the Latin language and word forms. Philippians 2:7, for example, was translated "but he exinanited himself." Such words were apt to be unintelligible to the average English reader, though entirely plain to an English Catholic priest.

The first Douay Bible was a purely private venture and not one "authorized" by the Roman Catholic Church. Eventually it was given official standing and is accepted today (after having undergone considerable revision) as the English version for use by Roman Catholics. Its roots, however, are in the Vulgate.

44   What was the Latin Vulgate?

The first Bibles used in the English churches were all written in Latin, and the priests were the only ones who could read them. This text was known as the Vulgate and was used by all Roman Catholic Churches.

45   What does "Vulgate" mean?

It comes from the same Latin root as our modern word "vulgar" and means "Common." The Vulgate was that version of the Bible which had been provided for the people in their common tongue (the language of the people as it was at that time) by the Roman Catholic Church. The production of such a Bible was the result of two great changes of language that had appeared in the life of the Christian Church.

46   How did the language change first?

As has already been suggested, Jesus preached and taught in Aramaic, the language which was commonly used in Palestine in his day. The first Christians were Jews, and of course they used the Aramaic in their worship services. Peter's sermon on the day of Pentecost was, almost certainly, preached in Aramaic.

Outside of Palestine, however, the language commonly used in the lands around the eastern half of the Mediterranean Sea was Greek. Because of having been born in a Greek-speaking land and having learned its language, many Jews appeared at the Temple feasts unable to speak either Hebrew or Aramaic; and in the New Testament we find a record of at least one synagogue in Jerusalem (Acts 6:9) where services were conducted in the Greek language for their convenience. Quite naturally Greek-speaking Jews who returned faithfully to the Temple of the feasts were among the most devout of the race, and to many of them the message of Jesus made a profound appeal because of its high spiritual tone. Many of those who united with the Church under the influence of Peter's sermon were devout Greeks (Acts 2:5-11), of whom the martyr Stephen was one.

The first Christian services were held in Aramaic, of course; but with the addition of Greek-speaking members to the Church, and more particularly as a result of the spread of the Christian movement into the Greek-speaking world, the use of

Greek language became more and more common. As the Jewish wing of the Church disappeared and the Gentile Church emerged, the Christian faith moved over almost entirely into the Greek world. Paul's letters were all written in Greek, and most scholars believe all the rest of the New Testament books (as also all Christian literature of the time) were likewise composed in Greek. Thus the first change of language took place even before any of the New Testament was written.

47 What was the second change of language?

The early Christians were a missionary-minded people and went with their message everywhere. Greek might be spoken in the east Mediterranean world, but Latin was becoming the common language in the western half of the Roman Empire, where Greek was practically unknown. We know that Paul had large plans for going as far west as Spain on a missionary tour (Romans 1:14; 15:24, 28). He was prevented from doing so by his arrest; but had he been able to carry out his plans, he would have found an altogether different language and civilization from that he found in Ephesus, for his Greek language would have been almost useless to him.

Thus as the Christian movement spread out into the Latin-speaking areas of the world, it became necessary to preach in Latin and to spread the Christian writings in Latin. This changeover began in the second Christian century, and it came to a climax in the year 405.

48 What happened in A.D. 405?

Various efforts had been made, by individuals, groups, and churches, to translate the Christian Scriptures into the Latin in use by thousands of Christians. Some of these translations had merit and others were badly done. This situation gave rise to a demand that an official translation be provided by the Church for the spiritual benefit of the people. Toward the close of the fourth century the task of producing such a translation was assigned to a great scholar named Jerome, who associated with him a group of the most competent scholars available. They reviewed the older Latin versions with care, comparing them with the best texts available in the Greek and Hebrew languages. The resulting translation was finally completed in

A.D. 405. Because it was in the language of the common people of that time, it came to be called the "Vulgate."

49 How was the Vulgate received?

In spite of the fact that the name of the greatest scholar of the age was associated with it, the translation came in for much criticism. The famous theologian Augustine questioned the necessity of such a translation, and in a letter to Jerome he said that the rendering of one text had "produced a riot." As we learned in the case of early English translations that the opposition was bitter and prolonged, so also it was in the case of the Vulgate. In the end it triumphed, however, and is the base today of the Bible in use by the Roman Catholic Church in every land in which it carries on its work.

50 Was the Old Testament also in Greek at this time?

The original writings which compose the Old Testament appeared originally in Hebrew, as we have already learned. With the spread of the authority of Philip of Macedon and his famous son, Alexander the Great, the Greek language followed the armies. It was their ambition to make all the world "a Greek colony."

Alexander founded the city of Alexandria, in Egypt. Being friendly to the Jews he encouraged them to settle there. Long before the time of Jesus it had become one of the greatest Jewish centers of the world, with a magnificent university and a vast culture springing up. The dates are not definitely recorded, and the facts are not all known, but sometime about 250 B.C. a group of Alexandrian Jewish scholars took it upon themselves to translate the Hebrew Book of the Law (Genesis, Exodus, Leviticus, Numbers, Deuteronomy) into Greek in order that it might be the more readily understood by the hundreds of thousands of Jews who lived outside of Palestine, and whose daily speech was Greek. Because of a tradition that seventy scholars made this translation, it was called the Septuagint. Greek translations of other books were made from time to time as they came to be accepted by the Jews as scripture, and in time the Old Testament as we know it today was in circulation in Greek. This entire body of literature came to be known as the Septuagint among the Christians, who read the Greek translation rather than the original Hebrew as their Old Testament.

51 Did Jerome translate from the Septuagint?

He did in many passages, because his instructions were explicit. He had been told to revise the Old Latin translations by comparison with the Greek. He personally came to consider the Hebrew text more accurate, but he stuck to the Greek version in some instances because to have followed the Hebrew might have "produced a riot." In the historical books, however, he felt free to translate directly from the Hebrew.

52 Why was this Latin version used in England?

Even at the time Jerome's Vulgate was issued, there were evidences of an impending split between Christianity in the West (represented by Rome) and Christianity in the East (represented by Constantinople). The East, begin predominantly Greek in its language and culture, was content with the Septuagint. The West, being predominantly Roman in its life and language, felt the need of the Bible in Latin. The split between the two came finally in the eleventh century, and thereafter the Vulgate became the only official version of the West. In the belief that they were protecting the purity of the Scriptures, the authorities of the Roman Church discouraged and forbade its translation into the national languages of the lands into which it went with missionaries. Thus, when the Douay translators came to make their version, they made it a literal translation of the Vulgate already in use in the English churches.

53 Was the King James Bible a translation of the Vulgate?

The first copy of the Bible to reach England with the missionaries sent out by Pope Gregory in A.D. 597 was the Vulgate version. Until Wycliffe, Tyndale, Coverdale, and others produced their translations, it was the only version of the Scriptures available to English readers. Being in Latin it was, of course, unintelligible to the average layman. This same situation was also true of all other nations in the West which had come under the influence of the Roman Catholic Church.

The first translators based their work, quite naturally, on the Vulgate; but as time went on and access was had to ancient manuscripts, the translators made use of them alongside the Vulgate. Some idea of the use made of such material can be guessed from the title page of the King James Version which reads as follows: "The Holy Bible, containing the Old and New Testaments, translated out of the original tongues; and with the former translations diligently compared and revised." This means that the King James Version was a new version and not merely a translation.

54 What is the difference?

A translation of the Vulgate would have been no more than a transfer of the ideas contained in Jerome's Bible from the Latin to the English. A new "version" means a Bible translated into the English in which the translators made use of the Latin Vulgate, of course, but all other available scripture manuscripts.

55 What were the manuscripts?

We need to be reminded that up to the time of Johann Gutenberg's invention of the printing press and the process of printing from movable type in the middle of the fifteenth century, all literature of every kind was produced by hand. Any copy of any portion of the Scriptures remaining to us from before that time is therefore known as a manuscript—"written by hand." Publishing in that early day was a very interesting and expensive business.

56 How did the ancients publish books?

This can be best illustrated by the story of the publication of the Bible which was ordered by Emperor Constantine, the first Christian emperor of Rome. Convinced that it would be of great advantage to the Christian Church, and hoping to enrich his own fame, he ordered the publication of an "edition" of the Bible. A publisher engaged a large hall and hired a company of scribes. Each scribe was equipped with parchment, pens, inkstands, low table, and all other necessary material. A reader sat at a desk at the head of the room somewhat in the fashion of a schoolmaster. He would read a word, a phrase, or a sentence, and each scribe would copy it down on the page in front of him.

This done, another phrase would be read and copied, and then another. In the course of time the entire Bible had been copied thus and each scribe had produced a pile of sheets. These would be bound together into a single volume. The number of books thus produced would depend of course upon the number of scribes employed.

57 Was this an efficient method of publishing?

The accuracy of the different volumes varied according to the skill and accuracy of the individual scribes. One poor penman might make a bad copy, full of mistakes, and another penman—skillful and careful—might produce one that was much more nearly accurate. Moreover, it was the habit of all penmen to develop their own systems of abbreviations, and the reader would find it necessary to accustom himself to the individual style of the scribe who did the copying.

58 Was the Vulgate published in this manner?

It was, both in its original form as it came from the hand of Jerome and his associates, and in subsequent editions which were copied from his original. The result was that, no matter how accurate the first edition may have been, its successors included variations from the original text which had been produced under the watchful eye of Jerome. It was inevitable that the Vulgate in use in the English churches should have been a more or less corrupted text, for many errors would almost certainly creep in between the first issuance of Jerome's translation in A.D. 405 and the time of Wycliffe's English translation toward the close of the fourteenth century.

59 Was the Douay Bible a version or a translation?

It was a translation, for it undertook to do nothing more than bring the Vulgate over into the English. The modern "revision" of the Roman Catholic Bible is, however, a new "version," for the scholars who have translated it have consulted the best ancient manuscripts available to them. While they have followed Jerome's translation in most instances, they have not hesitated to include accredited facts and findings which research has brought to light. There is, however, another difference which is of very great importance and which represents the outworking of a principle of much significance.

24

60   What is that additional difference?

The original Douay translation was designed for the use of the clergy, who were presumed to be familiar with Latin. The English text therefore followed the Latin very closely—sometimes slavishly—so much so that the lay reader found it difficult to understand. The modern translation offered to the people by the Roman Catholic Church is designed for the use of the laity and departs from the Latin again and again in an effort to accommodate itself to the common speech of the common people. In this respect the more recent of both Protestant and Catholic "revisions" of the Scripture agree.

61   What is the reason for revisions?

One very important reason is that languages change with the passing of the years. Words which meant one thing in one generation come to mean something else to a later generation. For example, in Ephesians 2:13, as it was translated in 1611, certain Gentiles were addressed as "ye who sometimes were far off"—which today gives the impression that the people under discussion oscillated back and forth, and just occasionally reached considerable distance. But in 1611 the word "sometimes" had a quite different meaning, which to King James and his contemporaries conveyed the correct idea of "formerly," making the sentence refer to the one great experience of their conversion from paganism to faith in Christ. An even more striking example is the request of Salome that King Herod give her "by and by in a charger the head of John the Baptist." According to modern understanding of the phrase she seems to be in no hurry for her prize to be delivered; and we wonder why the king, since he is "exceeding sorry" about the matter, did not wait till he could think up some way to save the prophet. But back in 1611 "by and by" meant almost exactly the opposite from what it means today. So Salome was really demanding the prophet's head at once rather than at the king's convenience. Therefore, no matter how well the King James translators may have done their work, this changing in the sense of words has a tendency to outmode their version. However, there is an even more important reason for revisions.

62   What is this more important reason?

Increasingly over the years scholarly investigations and archaeological researches have made available many ancient manuscripts and other documentary materials which throw light on the exact meaning of the scriptures. Inscriptions on ancient walls, cooking utensils, monuments, official documents, and other historical finds have their contribution to make. A revision of the Bible, to be strictly accurate and entirely honest with the original authors, must take all such facts into careful consideration.

63   Did the King James translators do good work?

They did an excellent piece of work—so splendid indeed that the King James Version of the Bible has become during the more than three hundred years of its popularity the most formative and creative influence in English literature. But however good the work may have been, and no matter how perfect its English style, the fact that new light has been thrown upon the scripture text in recent years is not to be ignored. Such a discovery, for example, as the Egyptian crocodile is of the utmost importance.

64   What about the Egyptian crocodile?

For many years scholars had noted the fact that the Greek text of the New Testament was something quite different from the classical Greek employed by the great Greek authors. Various explanations were offered, but not until a stuffed crocodile was unearthed in Egypt was the matter cleared up. In excavating an ancient Egyptian temple the workers came upon a mounted crocodile which served as a decoration. In the process of moving it the workmen accidentally broke it open, whereupon it was discovered that the ancient taxidermist had stuffed it with old papers consisting of bills of sale, personal letters, public documents, and a variety of similar material.

65   How does this relate to the New Testament?

When the scholars began investigating, they discovered that these scraps of writing were in the same Greek style as that employed in the New Testament. This proved conclusively that the New Testament scriptures were written by men who were primarily concerned in putting their message into the speech of the common people. Instead of using the "classical" style they used the popular vocabulary and manner of speech. It was like what we might call "newspaper English."

66 Is this very significant?

It is significant in at least two respects. First, the original writers quite evidently were more interested in getting their message to the people than in preparing a literary masterpiece. Accordingly, if modern translators are to be faithful to their trust, they will attempt to get the scriptures into the speech of the common people. There is great value, of course, in a dignified style and good literary form. But if it ever becomes necessary to choose between the two, the scholars who revise the scriptures have ample justification for taking the vernacular instead of the classical style.

In the second place, the study of these ancient documents that came out of the crocodile (and thousands of others that were brought to light subsequently) revealed the fact that a really correct translation of the scriptures must take account of many idioms and phrases which had a popular meaning for the people of that time. The slang expression "I'll tell the world," in common use today, conveys an exact meaning to the teen-ager and the newspaper reader; but if it were to be read by someone a hundred years from now, it might convey an altogether different impression. Similarly, the vernacular Greek was a language quite different from the classical speech, and calls for a translation all its own.

67 What interest does the modern reader have in all this?

We must remind ourselves that the Hebrew in which the Old Testament was composed, and only to a slightly lesser degree the Greek of the New Testament, are dead languages. They have not been in everyday use by plain people for centuries. Idioms, slang, popular expressions, and even the classical forms of the ancient tongues must be studied with very great care in order to determine the exact meanings the words were intended to convey to the original readers. Such a study of a dead language calls for expertness of the highest order. Obvious the ordinary person cannot make such investigations, but must rely upon experts who make it their life work.

68 What attitude should we as modern readers take?

We should take the same attitude toward good scholarship in the biblical field that we take toward scholarship in any field. We want our physicians to know the latest facts and theories in the field of medicine; we should want our preachers and Bible teacher to know and use the latest facts and developments in the field of Bible study. In other words, we should take a scientific attitude toward the Bible.

69 What is that scientific attitude?

Whenever a scientist lays bare a fact in the field of medicine, for example, all medical people are grateful. When enough facts have come to light, they can explain that which has been a mystery. Any fact is absolutely impartial, and no one serves the cause of truth by ignoring facts. If anything is true, or if it is a fact, God gave it its "trueness" or God made it a fact. We never honor our Lord by shutting our eyes to facts, though we may be able to win arguments in that way.

70 Must every reader of the Bible be a scholar?

By no means. But every reader of the Bible will find it of very great advantage to make use of the facts and the knowledge which scholars have put at his disposal. The Bible makes reference, for example, to many historical situations. Unless we know something about those situations we cannot understand what the Bible writers said. It often happens that the Bible gives no such information, and it must be sought in many fields.

71 Are all Bible scholars trustworthy?

Just as some physicians are unreliable, for any one of several reasons, so also some biblical scholars may be unreliable. But the mountebank in medicine is soon discovered, and in similar fashion the pretender in the biblical field is identified sooner or later.

72 How can we check on them?

They are constantly checking on one another. The average scholar works alone and is free to arrive at independent opinions. These opinions are then submitted to other researchers, and they test them in the light of all the facts at their command. Some of them may have other facts not available to the originator of the opinion under investigation. Perhaps those facts support the opinion, or perhaps they show it to be false. If the new idea can stand up under investigation, it is accepted; if it collapses, it is discredited.

Suppose, for example, that one scholar comes to the conclusion that a certain psalm was composed for a certain old Hebrew festival, and publishes an article to that effect. Then suppose another scholar unearths facts showing that the psalm was in use long before the festival was inaugurated. Obviously the first one would have to admit the error.

73 Are the scholars all agreed concerning the Bible?

Certainly not in all matters. In the case of the great basic principles they are, of course, and it is extremely interesting to discover the widespread tendency for them to come to agreement in matters which were under sharp dispute only a few years or decades ago. In general it might be said, however, that they are most nearly agreed regarding the recovery of the accurate text from the manuscripts.

74 What is the problem about the manuscripts?

We have already noted (Questions 55-57) that before the invention of printing in the fifteenth century every copy of every book had to be written by hand. Any individual who wants to test his own ability as a scribe will soon discover that it is practically impossible to copy a substantial amount by hand without making some mistakes. Ancient scribes made their share of mistakes; and after a copy was separated from its original, attempts to correct them might introduce new errors. Thus when the scholars today compare the scripture manuscripts, they find hundreds and even thousands of details in which each one varies from the others. Their problem is to determine which of the several different readings of a certain word or phrase is the correct copy of the originals.

75 Are there no originals to go by?

So far as we know there are no original manuscripts in

existence, just as they came from the pen of the author. Everything we have with which to work has been copied, sometimes from other copies only a little older and sometimes quite evidently copied from others much older.

76 Is the oldest therefore most accurate?

It might seem logical to assume that the older a manuscript is, the nearer it is to the original; and in general this is true. But not necessarily. For example, a very imperfect copy could have been made of the original, and then it could have been hidden away and not come to light until centuries afterward. Its age would not make it a faithful reproduction. Another copy, much more perfect, might have been made at the same time which came into wide use and in time wore out with another excellent copy being made from it. In the course of time several copies of copies could appear, each one representing careful work on the part of the copyist. Eventually a copy of the fourth or fifth generation might be compared alongside the imperfect copy of the first generation which had been in hiding. Obviously, the "younger" copy would be preferable because it was more nearly a perfect reproduction of the original. All this suggests that the study and evaluation of the ancient manuscripts is a science of its own.

77 What happened to the originals?

The Magna Charta, that great English document upon which rests our modern doctrine of civil rights, was penned and signed on June 15, 1215. It was deposited in the archives of the British government, but in time it began to fade in spite of the best care that could be given it. Thereupon a copy was made, also by hand. In time this also began to fade, for ink and paper are both perishable. The visitor to the British Museum today will be shown a series of "editions" or "copies" of the immortal document, all of which are illegible, not because of any fault on the part of any copyist but due to perfectly natural causes. In the same way the original Bible manuscripts passed out of use, or became illegible, and were replaced by copies, which in turn had to be replaced by newer copies and still newer copies. There is a difference, however, in that none of the early Bible manuscripts seem to have been laid away in archives for safekeeping. Instead, they were all put to rather vigorous use that would wear them out quickly and subject them to the risk of damage. In fact there are evidences in certain parts of the Bible that some original manuscripts may have suffered damage before any copies were made of them.

78 What damage might occur?

The most likely damage would be the breaking or tearing off of the first or last page of a book, since these pages would naturally receive the hardest treatment. Scholars are inclined to suspect this in any case where a book begins or ends with unexplainable abruptness, but the most probable instance is the ending of the Gospel of Mark.

79 What about the ending of Mark?

In the most trustworthy manuscripts the Gospel of Mark ends with 16:8, leaving the resurrection story rather obviously incomplete. Verses 9-20 as found in the King James Version come from late manuscripts, and the scholars are generally agreed that they were added sometime during the second century or after as an attempt to supply a substitute for what was missing. The matter is treated in more detail in Study No. 12 of this series, and it is enough to note here that the most likely explanation is damage to the final page of the original manuscript or an early copy. It should be noted also, however, that another sort of damage might occur.

80 What other sort of damage is that?

Anyone who has ever examined the Bible on the pulpit of his church—if it is a book that has been in use through many years—will have noticed that some pages are badly worn, and some have been torn out and, perhaps, thrust back into the book entirely out of place. Unless the pages were numbered it would be almost impossible to get them all back in order.

Among the early Christians there were few books, and such as they had were not expertly constructed as are our modern books. Pages were not numbered, and in some instances all the writing had not been done by the same penman. Thus, for a variety of reasons, when the pages became disarranged, it was extremely difficult to get them back into their original order. With numerous individuals consulting the books, or reading from them, it is easy to understand that some might handle them carelessly. This seems to explain a very interesting fact concerning the two books of Corinthians in our modern New Testament.

81 What about the Corinthian letters?

When we come to investigate Paul's letters to the Corinthians in Study No. 8, we will discover that there is good evidence that the material consisted, originally, of three (or perhaps even four) letters from the great Apostle. If this is true, it can be explained by the fact that some church owned copies of the various letters, and as they became worn some person (either carelessly or ignorantly) patched them together improperly. Then when they were copied, the copyist was unaware of the fact that the pages were out of order, and he copied them as they appeared in the pasted form, thus perpetuating the error.

82 On what material was the Bible first written?

The first material specifically prepared for writing that we have any knowledge of was the clay tablet, which was baked hard after letters had been pressed into it with a wedge-shaped reed. It is possible that some early passages of the Old Testament may have been written on such tablets when first composed. No tablets containing any scripture text have yet been discovered, but there are tablets from early Old Testament times which contain information of great value to the scholars in their efforts to understand the precise meaning of certain passages of scripture. It seems more likely, however, that the books of the Bible were first written on a more convenient sort of material—the papyrus roll.

83 What is a papyrus roll?

An odd three-cornered reed grew in Egypt in great abundance. This papyrus plant was smooth outside, and inside it was filled with a pith which would act as a glue when layers of the reed were subjected to pressure. Perhaps as early as 2500 B.C. the Egyptians discovered that by stripping the reeds and laying them correctly they could produce a relatively smooth sheet of writing material much like modern paper. To make enough for a book they pasted sheets of this material together into a long strip and rolled it on a stick somewhat after the fashion of a modern windowshade. The size of such a roll (or scroll, as it is often called) might vary, but in general it would measure about twenty feet in length and about sixteen inches in width.

84 Were all Bible books written on scrolls?

Although the papyrus roll seem to have been an Egyptian monopoly for many centuries, it eventually came into use throughout the Middle East and the Mediterranean area. Probably it was being used in Palestine from at least the time of David, about 1000 B.C. Therefore it is highly probable that the first Old Testament writings of any length were inscribed on papyrus rolls. It is quite possible, however, that some of the books were written on parchment as methods of making this more durable material from the hides of sheep were developed. Nevertheless, whether papyrus or parchment, the word "book" wherever it appears in the Bible always means a scroll. So far as we can tell, it was not till after the New Testament was written that the codex book came into common use.

85 What is a codex?

"Codex" is the Latin word for the modern form of book with leaves bound together along one edge. Papyrus sheets would not hold up very well in this form, and it appears that codex books were not often used till someone invented an improved process for making parchment of exceptional quality for writing purposes—what is known today as vellum. The change-over from scrolls to codexes seems to have begun soon after the New Testament was completed, with the result that most of the scripture manuscripts that have survived to this day are vellum codexes.

86 How many manuscripts do we have today?

There are available to the modern scholar about five thousand manuscripts of the Greek and Hebrew texts, some of which are no more than mere fragments and others of which are complete or nearly complete Bibles. A large portion of them have come to light since the King James Version was completed in 1611, which means that today's scholar has a great advantage over the "learned men" who gave us our early English Bibles.

87 Are they all valuable?

All have value because each one contributes some evidence in the search for the correct text, even though it may help with only one verse. But they are far from being of equal value. Those which are complete or nearly complete are of course much more valuable than mere fragments, and the manuscripts that go back to the very early centuries are valuable beyond any estimate. Thus our three oldest copies of what were originally complete Bibles are priceless treasures.

88 Where is the oldest copy of the Bible?

The oldest known copy, called the Codex Vaticanus, is owned by the Roman Catholic Church and is preserved in the Vatican at Rome. It consists of seven hundred pages of sheepskin, each of which is about one foot square. Some chapters of Genesis are missing, also some of the Psalms, and that portion of the New Testament which follows Hebrews 9:14. It is in a rather remarkable state of preservation and can be read quite easily by those who are skilled in such matters. The scholars believe it dates from the fourth century, which means that it was in existence in Jerome's day. There is an interesting conjecture set forth by some of them, which can be no more than a conjecture, that it may have been one of the fifty Bibles known to have been ordered by Constantine, the first Roman emperor to accept Christianity (see Question 56).

89 What is the next oldest?

This honor is generally accorded to Codex Sinaiticus, so called because it was found in 1844 in a monastery located at the foot of Mount Sinai. The story of its find is an extremely interesting one, in which a famous German archaeologist named Tischendor discovered the monks using pages of it for scratch paper, not knowing its value. About half the Old Testament had been used up in this fashion. The Russians owned it for years, but in 1935 it was sold to the British government for $500,000 and is preserved today in the British Museum in London.

90 What is the third?

Codex Alexandrinus, also the property of the British government and housed in the British Museum, is believed to come from the fifth century. It is complete except for a few scattered pages. Because it is so nearly complete, it is in many ways our most valuable document. It must be remembered, however, that these three manuscripts, like all the other early copies of the complete Bible, are entirely in Greek. The Old Testament in them is a translation rather than the original Hebrew text.

91 Where were the Hebrew manuscripts?

From the second century till the invention of printing in the fifteenth, Christian scholars read the Old Testament in Greek and Latin; and hardly a handful followed the example of Jerome in studying the Hebrew text. Thus all the Hebrew manuscripts were copied and recopied by Jewish scribes. They worked with the utmost care, even counting the letters to check against any omissions. But they followed a peculiar custom which has kept us from possessing any but very late manuscripts.

92 What was that peculiar Jewish custom?

Just as the patriot holds the flag in great respect and endeavors to protect it against all profanation, so the ancient Jews revered their scriptures. When a roll in use in the synagogue became badly worn, a copy was made and the old one was burned to save it from the possibility of being treated disrespectfully. The general result of this practice is that none of their manuscripts dating from earlier than the tenth century have been preserved. Until the sensational discovery of the Dead Sea scrolls in 1947 we had only small fragments of the Hebrew text that had not been copied and recopied for a thousand years.

93 Wht are the Dead Sea scrolls?

In the summer of 1947 an antique dealer informed the head of the Syrian St. Mark's Monastery in Jerusalem that some Arab shepherds were proffering for sale certain rolls which had the appearance of being very old. Suspecting they might be valuable, he made the purchase and then sought expert advice about them. Because of unsettled political affairs they were shown to only a limited number of people until February, 1948, when a monk was sent to consult the American School of Oriental Research, also in Jerusalem. It happened at the moment that the director was away and his post was entrusted to a brilliant young American scholar named John C. Trever. Fortunately he was highly skilled in handling ancient manuscripts, and almost from his first glimpse at the rolls he recognized that they were of exceptional value. Further investigation convinced him that they were genuine Hebrew manuscripts from ancient times. Because they had been found in the neighborhood of the Dead Sea, they have been given the name "Dead Sea scrolls."

94   How were they discovered?

As the story was told by the Arabs, some boys were herding goats among the limestone hills, and in an effort to turn some of them a stone was thrown. It disappeared into a crevice on the side of the hill, and the sound of breaking stoneware was heard. Examination revealed the fact that the crevice opened into a cave in which a large number of earthen jars were stored. In breaking into the cave the boys destroyed some of the jars, but others were saved and were found to contain rolls of manuscript.

95   Who put the scrolls in the cave?

It is known that many Jewish sects were in existence during the first century A.D., somewhat as there are numerous Protestant bodies today. Each one stressed its own doctrine and carried on its own worship. Some of these are known to have been highly secretive, and many held their services in the hills and on the desert. John the Baptist may have been a member of one such. In the absence of any historical information to the contrary, scholars are inclined to believe that the Dead Sea scrolls were the property of some such sect which hid them away in the cave shortly before the Roman army under Titus destroyed Jerusalem in A.D. 70. This would have been only a generation later than the time of Christ. Members of the sect may have died in the defense of the city of Jerusalem without leaving any record or trace of their treasure hidden in the cave.

96   How do we know they are genuine?

Dr. Trever was an expert photographer and secured the

permission of the Syrian monks to photograph the rolls inch by inch. These pictures, together with his own translations, were sent to leading American authorities, who confirmed his opinion. Considerable controversy raged over the matter for a time, but they are accepted today as being authentic. As such they are conceded to be the oldest biblical manuscripts of any length now known to exist.

97 How old are they?

They are believed to have been copied from some older manuscript probably sometime during the first century before Christ.

98 What do they contain?

The complete book of Isaiah and two of the three chapters of the book of Habakkuk, with fragments of one or two other scriptural books. Other rolls contain nonscriptural writings that are nevertheless highly valuable in shedding light on biblical history. One roll contains the text of the ancient book of Lamech, which until the discovery of the Dead Sea scrolls was believed to have passed completely out of existence.

99 What contribution do they make?

The Isaiah scroll has been compared word for word with the Hebrew texts already available, in order to note all the variations. Since a thousand years of copyings separates them, we might expect a considerable number of changes. Actually there are no more differences than might be found in any two manuscripts. This rather reassures us that the whole Old Testament was probably copied with equal care during this thousand years.

100 Will any more such rolls be found?

It is impossible to answer this question with any degree of satisfaction because of the unsettled political situation which prevails in the Middle East. Several scientific organizations are interested in the work, the Roman Catholic Church has some highly skilled specialists on the field, and important finds could be announced at almost any time. The Bedouins know that a good price will be paid for such rolls, and they are apt to be very careful that nothing is destroyed. But the prospect of good sales also increases the hazard that spurious material may be offered for sale.

101 Are the manuscripts available to all Bible students?

For many years ancient Bible manuscripts were available only to the favored few for the reason that they were very fragile and it was necessary to protect them against frequent handling. In recent years, however, all of the most important ones have been carefully photographed, page by page, and these pictures are now available to anyone interested in studying them. For example, Dr. Trever's color photographs of the Dead Sea scrolls are a treasure of the utmost importance, and from them he has lectured before many audiences. Theological schools and learned societies are quite familiar with them. This means that there are no secrets connected with any of them; all are available to students capable of making a scientific study of them. It is impossible therefore for anyone to practice any deceptions in connection with them.

102 Did the manuscripts require a revision of the King James Version?

They made a major contribution to the necessity, but they did not cause it alone. As has already been suggested, no one reads the King James Version today precisely as it was published in 1611. The spellings of many words have changed with the passing of the years. As an example, there is the well-known verse from the Twenty-third Psalm which, in the first edition of the King James Version, appeared thus: "The Lord is my shepheard; I shall not want. He maketh me to lie downe in greene pastures." Then there is the equally well-known phrase from Paul's immortal thirteenth chapter of First Corinthians: "Charitie vaunteth not itselfe, is not puffed vp." Then, too, some differences of opinion concerning what was and what was not scripture had their effect. In 1629, just eighteen years following the first appearance of the King James Version, an edition appeared from which the Apocrypha were omitted. This was a revolutionary alteration, as will be made clear later in this study. At any rate, it indicates that the translators believed they had a moral right to take some liberties with the text, based on their godly judgment. Numerous revisions have appeared in the course of the years, and yet some errors remain in the text. For example, the text of Matthew 23:24 reads "strain *at* a gnat" whereas the original Greek, as well as the earlier English versions, make it very plain that "strain *out* a gnat" is the correct wording.

103 Did these revisions make any radical changes?

As was stated in the preceding answer, the omission of the Apocrypha was a radical departure from the accepted text. How radical it was will be explained in more detail when we come to a study of the attitude of the Jews toward the Apocrypha, as also that of the early Christian Church. But the other revisions which appeared between 1611 and 1769 represented little more than the opinions of individuals or small groups. They served little purpose except to call attention to the fact that the language kept outgrowing the Bible.

During relatively recent years, however, there have been three thorough revisions which claimed some sort of authorization from accredited Protestant groups: (1) the Revised Version, which Americans generally call the English Revised Version; (2) the American Standard Version; and (3) the Revised Standard Version. In addition there have been numerous individually sponsored translations.

104 What about these individual translations?

Almost from the time of the first appearance of the King James Version there have been those individual scholars who have published translations which they have hoped would make a contribution to our general understanding of the Scriptures. In most of such cases reliance has been placed on expressive phrases, telling speech, or modern words to make the meaning clearer. Perhaps the most popular of these today is known as the Moffatt Bible. It includes both the Old and the New Testament as translated by Dr. James Moffatt. Another popular one is the American Translation, consisting of an Old Testament section translated by a Hebrew scholar named J. M. P. Smith, with the assistance of several associates, and a New Testament which is the work of the famous Greek scholar Edgar J. Goodspeed. There are perhaps a score or more of others which have been produced by highly reputable scholars, but these will suffice to illustrate the case.

105 What is the English Revised Version?

While it is true that changes in spelling and the alterations of the meanings of words necessitated various minor revisions from time to time, a much more important reason for revising the English Bible appeared in the accumulation of old manuscripts such as have already been described. Nearly a hundred individual translations of one sort and another, and of widely varying worth, had appeared between 1611 and 1870.

On February 10, 1870, the Convocation of Canterbury of the Church of England heard a proposal that there should be a new "authorized" revision of the English Bible, and after debating the matter for many months it gave its approval. A company of English scholars of the highest rank and authority were chosen, not all of whom were members of the Anglican Church. In this respect, at least, the work was not the product of a single church body, but the action of the convocation gave it the utmost authority, at least so far as the Established Church was concerned. These scholars spent years in a thoroughgoing revision of the text. At length, on May 17, 1881, the Revised Version of the New Testament was published, the Old Testament following on May 19, 1885.

106 How was the Revised Version received?

The new Bible had a great reception at first, more than a million copies of the New Testament having been ordered in advance. A total of three million copies were sold in Great Britain and the United States during the first year. On May 20, 1881, the book was placed on sale in the United States and two Chicago newspapers printed it in its entirety in their issues two days later.

107 What is the American Standard Version?

Associated with the British committee preparing the Revised Version was a group of American scholars who were consulted from time to time, but who did not have the right to vote on disputed matters. When the complete text was published, a partial list of their suggestions was included in something like

40

an appendix. They had an agreement with the British committee almost from the start, however, that they would produce later a revision for the American public in which they would have free right of way to express their own judgments. In order that the two might not seem to compete it was agreed that the American edition should not appear until at least fourteen years following the appearance of the English Revised Version. In accordance with that agreement the American Standard Version was presented to the public on August 26, 1901. Its reception at the hands of the public was generally favorable, but far less spectacular than that which attended the English revision.

108 Was the American Standard Version "authorized"?

There was no organized body of Protestantism in America during the last quarter of the nineteenth century which was competent to "authorize" any translation or revision. The committee which undertook the work can be said to have represented the scholarship of American Protestantism, but the American Standard Version lacked the "authorization" which had been given the English Revised Version.

109 Why is it called "Standard"?

The popularity of the English Revised Version, as well as the interest aroused by the appendix and the promise of an American version, proved too strong a temptation to certain publishers. They put out editions of the Revised Version which incorporated in the text the changes that had been listed in the appendix of the English edition, with other changes secured from individual American scholars, and entitled them "American Revised Version." These editions caused no little confusion to the public, who supposed them to be the promised work of the formally organized committee which had worked with the British revisers. Accordingly when the authentic version was issued, it was labeled "Standard"; and it was copyrighted in order to protect it and the Bible-reading public.

110 Who owns the copyright?

In 1928 it was turned over to the International Council of

Religious Education, the co-operative body which for many years had been selecting the Sunday-school lessons for the major Protestant denominations. This body merged in 1951 with four other great interdenominational agencies to form the National Council of the Churches of Christ in the United States of America, which represents the co-operation of most of the Protestant churches of the country.

111 What is the Revised Standard Version?

Immediately on receiving the copyright of the American Standard Version the council appointed a committee of scholars to look after it. This committee investigated the use of the version, and criticisms of it, and in 1930 proposed that a complete new revision be undertaken. After seven years of study and debate the project was given final approval, and was launched, with a committee of translators representing many denominational interests and viewpoints. Then followed more yers of research and discussion as the scholars prepared the translation. At length on February 11, 1946, the Revised Standard Version of the New Testament was presented to the public. The Old Testament section required six years longer. On September 30, 1952, the Revised Standard Version of the entire Bible was offered to the public in a series of more than three thousand great municipal rallies across the nation.

112 Is the new version copyrighted?

It is. The experience of the English Revised Version made it appear that the public should be protected against fraud, and to copyright the book seemed the only way to do so.

113 Is the Revised Standard Version an "authorized" version?

It is, insofar as any such authorization can be obtained from American Protestantism. There are individuals, congregations, and particular groups which do not accept it as being authorized, just as the Puritans did not accept the King James Version. But it has been produced under the authority of the National Council of Churches, which is the most representative body of American Protestantism in existence.

114   Does that end the matter of revisions?

By no means. In Great Britain, as the result of an initiation by the Church of Scotland, later endorsed by the Convocation of Canterbury on May 20, 1947, a committee of British scholars was organized. This time it is representative of all the major denominations and is instructed to study procedures and plans for a new English revision. No publication date has been set, but that a new revision will be produced seems almost certain.

The Roman Catholic Church, following its own line of research and scholarship, is in the process of producing a new revision of its Douay Bible (see Question 57) for English and American readers. The work is very well done indeed, and is enjoying wide favor among the faithful. A great change has taken place since the day when Wycliffe's bones were exhumed and burned, and today from American Catholic pulpits the people are urged to read their Bible.

115   How should we read the Bible?

There is a sense in which it can be said that the present arrangement of the text is unfortunate, for the earliest writings of neither Testament appear at the beginning. This makes little difference to the person who reads the Scripture for purely devotional purposes, for one can turn to the Psalms or the Gospels and read them for their inspiration quite apart from any interest in history or doctrine. If, however, one wishes to study the Scripture carefully and scientifically, it makes a great deal of difference. Perhaps it would be well to make some inquiry into the question of how we happen to have those books in the Bible which are actually there. Let us turn then to the question of the "canon."

116   What is the canon?

The word "canon," when applied to the Scripture, means "that which is accepted as being of sacred authority." But, as has been suggested, there are differences of opinion inside Christendom as to the authority of some of the religious writings of the Hebrews as well as some of the Christian books. Just as some excellent books were excluded from Dr. Eliot's five-foot shelf (see Question 2), so also numerous writings were excluded from the Bible.

117   Were they religious books?

The field which is opened up by this question is much too extensive to be studid in any satisfactory fashion in the brief space at our disposal, but it can be said that some of the books which did not win a place in the list of inspired books were of definite religious value. The Shepherd of Hermas, for example, which failed to gain acceptance into the New Testament, was in the opinion of many early Christians quite worthy of that high rank. In the field of the Old Testament a book called Ecclesiasticus is much more inspiring reading than Ecclesiastes, but that was not sufficient to enable it to win its place in the Hebrew scriptures.

118   Who selected the canon?

This question must follow one line for the Old Testament and another for the New Testament, for entirely different forces entered into the decisions in each case. The canon of the Old Testament was fixed by Jews and that of the New Testament was fixed by the Christian Church. It should be pointed out in this connection that almost as important as the question "Who wrote the books of the Bible?" is that other question, "Who chose the books of the Bible?"

119   Who decided the question of the New Testament?

No one person or group can be said to have chosen the books of the New Testament. Rather, over a period of several centuries there was continuing discussion throughout the Christian Church concerning the question of which books were to be regarded as being inspired. On the four Gospels and Acts there came to be general agreement at an early date; so also for the letters of Paul. But about the rest there was much variety of opinion, with one group of churches supporting certain books, and another favoring a different selection. When the canon was finally agreed upon (and it should be noted that at least two small remnants of ancient churches in the Middle East have still not agreed with the rest of Christendom about Revelation and several epistles), it was not by formal action but by actual use in the churches. Thus the members of the Christian Church in general chose the content of their New Testament.

120   Were there divisions in the Church then, as now?

Immediately after the stirring events of the Resurrection, Ascension, and Pentecost (Acts 2) the fire of the new evangel began to spread throughout the earth. Unfortunately we do not have any actual historical records except in the case of Paul and Peter (Acts of the Apostles), and the story of Peter is far from complete. There are legends and traditions concerning the travels of the others, but they are neither documented nor otherwise verified. In India there is a rather considerable body of Christians, known as the Orthodox Syrian Church of Malabar, who believe their church was founded by the Apostle Thomas, but the historical evidence is somewhat less than convincing. Travel then, as now, was common; and inasmuch as the Roman Empire had established something like a world order, it was relatively safe for traders, merchants, and missionaries to wander far. This had the effect of scattering the salt and within two hundred years flourishing churches were to be found in many lands.

121   Were they all a part of the Christian movement?

They were a part of the Christian movement, but they were not a part of any world-wide organization known as the Christian Church.

122   Was there no unified Christian organizations?

There was not. A variety of obstructions intervened, making a Christian Church almost an impossibility. In the first place the Christians were separated by language barriers. Something of this difficulty is suggested by the list of those who listened to the Pentecost sermon (Acts 2:9-11). Great distances separated the congregations, preventing them from developing any acquaintanceship or fellowship. Perhaps one of the most serious obstacles was the difference in racial cultures of the various congregations.

123   Were there any broad similarities?

By the end of the first Christian century a considerable body of Christian literature was in circulation among all the Christians. In time certain groupings developed, each one of which had some things in common, and these in time became churches.

124 What were some of these "groupings"?

Church historians speak of the Roman, Alexandrian, Syrian, Armenian, and one or two other "churches." By this they do not mean that they were entirely independent organizations, but rather that each was a number of congregations which were drawn together by ties of language, race, geography, or other natural interest. Then, in addition, we must reckon with the influence of powerful preachers, pastors, leaders, and scholars who appeared inside these groups to hold them together.

125 What did they have to do with the New Testament?

Each of the New Testament books came into existence quite independently, as the result of the religious concern of some individual. It can hardly be said that any church, or individual, sat down deliberately to write scripture. But once he had written his book and sent it out to be read, there were those who began to say it was "inspired." While none were written deliberately at the insistence of any church, all the churches everywhere contributed opinion which eventually resulted in the choices that fixed the canon.

126 Were they not in agreement?

It must be remembered that much literature developed among the early Christians. This was due to the fact that everyone was free to write if he chose to do so, and many individuals arose who held very positive convictions. No one had any idea he was writing scripture, but having ideas and feeling a sense of responsibility for expressing those ideas, he put them down in literary form. At no time did the Christian Church or its leaders commission anyone to write scripture.

127 Was the New Testament written then by accident?

There is a sense in which it can be said that this was the case. All Christians will probably agree that the Holy Spirit was guiding the writers, and history seems to show that God had a design at which he worked. But certainly it cannot be said that the early Christian Church set out to produce the New

Testament. For making that statement there is very good reason.

128 What is that good reason?

The first Christians were Jews. As such they accepted the doctrine of the divinely appointed Messiah who was to establish a new era among men as God's chosen representative. The early Christians, including the original disciples, believed profoundly that Jesus was the Messiah, but they were compelled to admit that he had not done the work commonly expected of the Messiah. Seizing upon some things Jesus had said, and some interpretations they had put on his words, they became convinced that he would return speedily, following his ascension, and take up the work where he had left it off. Because the first-century Christians believed profoundly in this doctrine (which bulked large in Paul's preaching), the thought that the Church was under any responsibility for producing a New Testament never entered their thinking. Because Jesus was to come again soon, no scripture would be needed. As another result of the same doctrinal belief, the leaders did not attempt to develop a world-wide organization which could have been called a "church." In the meantime a mass of Christian literature developed out of which the New Testament was finally selected.

129 Was the amount really considerable?

It must have been. First of all, there were all the books we now have in our New Testament. Then, in addition, there were several score of books, letters, and treatises to which reference is made in the early church records. Some of these have been preserved for us, but most of them have been irretrievably lost.

130 Was this literature widely circulated?

Paul's letters seem to have gone throughout the entire Christian community, as did also the four Gospels, Acts, and some of the general epistles. Quite a number of other books, such as the Shepherd of Hermas, also seem to have been known both in the East and in the West. On the other hand there were many writings of a religious character which were produced locally, and never got into general circulation. Even some books that finally got into the New Testament were more widely read in some parts of the Church than in others.

131 What books were these?

The book of Revelation is probably the best example. It was written by a Christian preacher who was imprisoned by the Roman government and confined on the dreary isle of Patmos. It was designed as a tract to encourage the Christians who were, just at that time, suffering the severities of Roman persecution. As we will discover in Study No. 11, Revelation had a great influence in steadying the Church and fortifying the Christians during the terrors of those days. As a consequence it was very highly esteemed in the West, where the persecutions were most severe. The churches of the East, including those in Egypt, did not suffer in the same way, with the result that Revelation did not come to mean the same to them, and they were less inclined to include it in their New Testament.

The Epistle to the Hebrews, on the other hand, enjoyed a fate quite the opposite. Lightly esteemed in the West, it was highly favored in the East. It is interesting to note that, though Jerome included Hebrews in the Vulgate, he made the comment that "the custom of the Latins does not accept it." Augustine likewise was hesitant about accrediting it as scripture. The two books in some measure continue in the same relationship to this day—Revelation popular in the Roman Catholic Church and Hebrews popular in the Greek Orthodox Church.

132 What gave rise to such differences of opinion?

There being no newspapers or magazines during those early Christian centuries while the Church was expanding, it was difficult for the various Christian leaders to compare their thinking. They never came together in any conference, and each one worked alone. Each man suffered from the lack of friendly and constructive criticism of other men equally competent. Thus it might happen that one leader would attract a great following in Alexandria and another leader would attract an equally great following in Rome, the two of them holding views quite divergent. The only way they could compare notes would be by writing letters—always less than satisfactory. Disparity of beliefs, a difference in emphasis, and varying viewpoints were inevitable.

133   When did the idea of a New Testament first appear?

Sometime toward the close of the first century the church at Ephesus seems to have made a collection of Paul's letters. This was published and distributed in some way, with the result that the idea of a compilation of letters took root in the thinking of the Church. At any rate, about A.D. 95 a Christian writer appropriated the idea and addressed what might be called a "circular letter" to the seven Christian congregations of Asia Minor and ascribed to it something of the character of scripture.

134   What was that "circular letter"?

The book of Revelation. It will be noted that the author addresses his work to the seven churches in his opening chapter (1:4), and that in his closing chapter (22:18) he warns against any tampering. His first three chapters consist of a series of brief messages to the congregations as an introduction to his message of triumphant faith. In this he made the boldest claim in behalf of his book of anything to be found in the New Testament.

135   Did not Paul claim divine authority for his writings?

He seems to have expected his readers to take some kind of divine authority for granted. In fact in certain instances he felt it necessary to relieve God of responsibility for some particular thing he said (I Corinthians 7:25-26; II Corinthians 11:17), lest they assume too much authority. In the first chapter of his letter to the Galatians he makes very positive claims for the divine origins of his message. Nevertheless there seems little reason to believe that he thought he was writing scripture. Rather he wrote his letters for a more specific purpose.

136   Why did Paul write his letters?

Many of the strong churches of both Europe and Asia owed their origins to Paul's preaching, and he held himself responsible for their nurture and growth. When he saw them developing dangerous tendencies, he felt it his duty to warn them, instruct them, or call them to account. In each instance his letters were written for the purpose of meeting a particular situation in a particular place. There is no trace of any anticipation that his letters would ever be included in such a book as the New Testament. Only in one or two instances did he seem to expect that a congregation other than the one to which they were addressed would read them.

137 How did they come to be read more widely?

A number of reasons required that they be read widely. The first Christian century was a period when there was much running to and fro over the earth by traders, politicians, merchants, and preachers of religious doctrines. The Christian congregations were very frequently hosts to travelers who professed the faith and who welcomed the opportunity to worship with other believers. Such persons, hearing one of Paul's letters read, and being impressed by its good sense or its spiritual value, frequently asked for permission to make copies which could be presented to other churches.

Each congregation had its own problem just as modern churches do; and visitors in strange cities, hearing some part of one of Paul's letters which applied to a situation "back home," might ask for a copy of that portion in order that it might be read to the home folk. In many such ways Paul's correspondence was given wide currency throughout the Christian world, especially in Europe and Asia Minor.

138 Were such letters received as scripture?

They were received and read as letters having behind them great authority. But during the first century no one ever suggested that there should be a body of Christian scriptures alongside the Hebrew scriptures. The Ephesian church (which seems to have been the first one to collect Paul's letters) was not attempting to choose scriptures; instead, it was interested in conserving the writings and counsel of the great Apostle. The concept of the New Testament was relatively slow in developing among the Christians.

139 Who started the idea?

About A.D. 140 a wealthy Greek shipowner named Marcion, from Sinope in Pontus, arrived at Rome with a collection of Christian writings which he proposed should be accepted by the Church as its book of scriptures. He was an extremely energetic layman without any particular religious training, who held certain violent prejudices. Partly for the purpose of promoting his personal viewpoint, and partly as a service to the Church, he prepared to publish his New Testament.

140 What were his prejudices?

He was bitterly anti-Jewish and strongly pro-Greek. He resented the fact that, as a Christian, he was expected to accept so much of Judaism, including the Old Testament. Being a proud Greek, and believing that Greek learning, literature, and culture were superior to anything else in the world, he had an ambition to see Christianity cut loose entirely from its Hebrew background. Thus it was largely for the purpose of making the Christian Church independent of the Hebrew Old Testament that he conceived the idea of a New Testament.

141 Of what did his New Testament consist?

In spite of himself Marcion continued to be greatly influenced by the Hebrew scriptures. It seems evident that he had the Law and the Prophets in mind when he proposed a New Testament to consist of a Gospel and Epistles. Because the Gospel of Luke had been written by a Greek convert to Christianity, it was chosen for the first place of honor. He then added ten letters of Paul. To correspond to the third division of the Hebrew scriptures, known as the Writings, he composed a book of his own and added it to the collection.

142 How was Marcion's New Testament accepted?

It enjoyed some small vogue for a time; but as the unsoundness of the Marcionite teachings began to be recognized, it lost favor. The basic idea of Christian scriptures became sufficiently rooted, however, so that it was only a short time until more thoughtful efforts were made to compile a New Testament which could be accepted by the entire Church.

143 Was there much Christian literature from which to choose?

There was nothing to prevent any zealous Christian from writing, if he was so disposed, and many were. Some wrote for the purpose of explaining their personal beliefs and some in the hope of converting pagans to a faith in Christ. Still others wrote believing they could influence the Church in matters of doctrine. The total result was a considerable body of literature.

144 Has any of it survived?

Aside from the twenty-seven books of our New Testament we have a limited number of Christian writings which have come down to us from the first and early second century. These are: the Epistle of Barnabus, the Shepherd of Hermas, the Revelation of Peter, the Teaching of the Apostles (the Didache), and letters of Clement of Rome, Ignatius, and Polycarp. Various other works are known by name, but their content can only be guessed at from the references later writers make to them.

145 Were such books called scripture?

Several of them were so called at one time or another, by one Christian group or another.

146 Were they ever included in any "New Testament"?

In Questions 88-90 we were introduced to the three old codexes known as Vaticanus, Sinaiticus, and Alexandrinus. They are the oldest manuscripts that have come down to us of what were originally complete copies of the Bible. They are believed to have come from Egypt and to have been published in the fourth and fifth centuries A.D. Vaticanus breaks off at Hebrew 9:14, and no one will ever know what may have been included from that point on. But Sinaiticus includes, in addition to the books in our modern New Testament, the Epistle of Barnabas and a part of the Shepherd of Hermas. Alexandrinus, likewise in addition to our New Testament books, includes I and II Clement following the Revelation of John, though II Clement is not complete. No one knows what may or may not have followed from those points on. Quite evidently all three books have suffered the loss of pages at the end of the New Testament.

147 What does all this prove?

These facts indicate that as late as the fifth century, probably in Egypt at least, there was no positive agreement as to which books should and which should not be included in the New Testament. The three codexes quite evidently served as the

Bibles of certain churches. Since they differed, it would seem to be true that there was a difference of opinion among the churches on the subject of the contents of the New Testament.

148 Was this disagreement widespread?

It must always be remembered that the Christians were scattered widely across the earth, that they spoke numerous languages and dialects, that each local church had its own leaders of whom few had ever had any formal training, and that during the early centuries there was no central organization or authority capable of saying what was and what was not standard practice or "orthodox" belief. Any Christian had as much right to say he represented the true faith as any other had; any church had as much right to choose the books it would regard as scripture as any other church had. It was inevitable, therefore, that there should be wide divergences of opinion. It is possible, however, to trace certain trends by studying the teaching and preaching of outstanding leaders.

149 What position did these leaders take?

A famous Christian named Justin was one of the conspicuous leaders of the church in Rome about A.D. 150. In one of his writings he says that the Christians of that city would gather on Sunday and listen to the reading of the memoirs of the apostles, or the writings of the prophets. By the "memoirs" he seems to have meant the four Gospels of our New Testament, and by the "writings of the prophets" he quite evidently meant the Old Testament. He did not describe the Gospels as being inspired, but the fact that they were read in the worship services indicates that they were on their way toward that status. Although he knew about the Pauline epistles, he nowhere intimates that they were to be considered as being inspired. They were read occasionally in the services, but not on the same level as the Gospels and the Old Testament. Justin's position, with slight variations, seems to have been the one taken by the most reputable leaders. From another source we have corroborating evidence.

150 What is that corroborating evidence?

In July of A.D. 180 a little group of Christians were on trial for

53

their lives in Scili in North Africa. Before the governor pronounced the sentence of death, he inquired of them concerning the contents of their church chest and was told that it contained "the books and the letters of Paul, a righteous man." It is agreed among the scholars that "the books" were very probably the Gospels and the Old Testament, and from the fact that Pauline letters were also to be found in the chest it is reasonable to assume that they were highly prized. Though they may not have been esteemed to be "inspired" in the same sense as the "books" were, they were at least on their way. In general this was probably true throughout the Church, though there were sects which held different opinions.

151 What about the sects?

It was inevitable that vagaries and strange doctrines should develop inside such a movement as Christianity, especially since there was no central authority to decide such issues. The second century saw many divergent groups spring up, any one of which was apt to take a different position relative to the scriptures. We know of one, at least, which completely rejected the Gospel of John. Because the followers of Marcion laid such great emphasis on Paul's letters, even these writings were for a time held under suspicion by the opposing party, which was the majority party. It was the conflict between the sects which finally compelled the Church to organize for the protection of the faith and an authoritative definition of doctrine. It is at this point that the Roman church emerged as a leader.

152 What about the leadership of the Roman church?

It enjoyed great prestige throughout Christendom because (1) it was led by some truly great churchmen, (2) it had never been taken over by any of the sects or heretics, and (3) it could trace its descent directly from the apostles. It was, therefore, in a position to lead the movement for unification. This movement toward a solidification of the Church into a coherent organization was spontaneous. It did not impose doctrines and practices upon the churches in any arbitrary spirit. Instead, it took those doctrines most commonly believed and those practices in most common use, and set them up as the standard for all.

153 How did this affect the New Testament?

The movement in the direction of the standardization of the Christian Church which developed during the closing decades of the second Christian century produced at least four definite reasons: (1) the Church began to be called "catholic"; (2) some general agreement developed concerning matters of doctrine to be commonly accepted; (3) worship forms (such as baptism) were harmonized; and (4) progress was made in the selection of those books which were to be called scripture by the Christians.

154 Upon what books did the Church agree?

In the year 1740 an Italian scholar named L. A. Muratori discovered a manuscript in Milan, Italy, which appeared to come from about the year 800, and which was a copy of an earlier document which must have been composed in Rome about A.D. 200. From it we get a clear picture of the New Testament as it was accepted in Rome at that time. Hebrews and the Epistles of James and Peter are omitted, but the list includes the Revelation of Peter and the Shepherd of Hermas, which do not appear in our New Testament. This "Muratorian Fragment" cannot be conclusive evidence, but it gives us valuable information showing that the mind of the Church was not yet made up concerning the question of the New Testament. For example, the Shepherd of Hermas is recommended for personal reading, but it is "not to be read publicly in church," because it was written too recently. It is admitted also that the Revelation of Peter is rejected by some. Only two Epistles of John are mentioned. It is assumed that this can be explained by the fact that two of the letters were combined in one, rather than that one was not accepted.

155 How was the matter finally settled?

In the process of getting the Church organized under one form of government, and with one standard statement of doctrine, a number of conferences were held to which leaders, preachers, scholars, and ecclesiastics came from far and near. For weeks at a time they discussed the various problems with which the Church was confronted, among those problems being the question of what was to be accepted as the official scriptures of Christianity. In the end there was general agreement that the New Testament as we have it today was to be approved. In doing so, two principles were followed.

156 What were those two principles?

Only those books were to be accepted which owed their origin (1) to apostolic authorship, including Pauline authorship, or (2) to the sponsorship or close influence of an apostle. Such a book as Mark, for example, which was actually written by John Mark was accepted because it was believed to have been written by the authority of Peter. Hebrews, long debated, was accepted on the basis that it was of Pauline authorship. But perhaps more to the point is the fact that the mind of the Church had gradually come to rather general agreement as the books had been in use in the worship services of the congregations. People were more inclined to believe claims of apostolic authorship for books they had found inspiring.

157 Was there any formal action in the case?

There was not. When Jerome was commissioned to translate the scriptures into Latin toward the close of the fourth century, he was given certain instructions, and at the same time he was allowed some discretion. Combining his own judgment with that of the Church as he knew and understood it, he translated the New Testament as we have it today, although there were those who, for hundreds of years afterward, believed that other books besides those he translated should also be included.

158 What were those "other books"?

Several received the support of one or another authority inside the Church. The Shepherd of Hermas was believed to be scripture by several great leaders of the Church during those early centuries, as were also the Revelation of Peter and the Epistle of Barnabus. The Teaching of the Apostles and Clement's letter to the Corinthians, together with a second writing attributed to Clement, made bids for acceptance but were finally rejected. The Epistle to the Laodiceans is one of the most interesting examples. This work, a crude and obvious imitation of a Pauline letter, kept cropping up. The author of the Muratorian Fragment rejected it entirely, saying that it was a forgery; but around A.D. 600 Pope Gregory the Great thought

56

it was a genuine Pauline document, though not necessarily scripture, and as late as the sixteenth century a leading French scholar took it seriously. Some of the other works continued to exercise influence for several hundred years. No one body of Christendom accepted them all, but all had the support of some very reputable and responsible Christians.

159 What is the meaning of all this?

In the life and thinking of Christians the New Testament exercises vast authority because of the belief that it is inspired. By this it is meant that divine sanction is behind the authors. But our studies thus far have made it very clear that even though a book might have been inspired, it had to run the gauntlet of use and experience. It seems, then, that the doctrine of inspiration must be defined in broad terms if it is to cover the entire situation; for if inspired writers wrote the New Testament, those who chose the twenty-seven books of which it is constituted must also have been inspired if they were to make intelligent and discriminating choices. This principle applies with equal force to the Old Testament, from which the early Christians learned the idea of inspired scripture.

160 How did the early Christians regard the Old Testament?

Alongside the life and teachings of Jesus, the Old Testament was the rock base of the early Christians' faith. Jesus had been reared in the tradition of the Jews, to whom the scriptures were of first importance. Whenever Jesus mentioned the scriptures, he was referring to the Old Testament, or some portion thereof. As the Christian movement spread over the world, it carried the Old Testament along.

161 Was that Old Testament the same as ours today?

There is a sense in which it can be said that the Old Testament in the first Christian century was the same as ours of today, but this statement needs some clarification. It contained all those books we have in our Old Testament, but there were in addition certain books which were on a debated list. To get the picture clear we must understand the divided opinion among the Jews themselves.

162 How was opinion divided among the Jews?

The little land of Palestine had not been large enough to provide a home for all of the Jews for several hundred years. Literally millions of them were scattered throughout the Roman world. The few thousands who returned from the Babylonian exile to rebuild Judah and Jerusalem were no more than a fraction of the total number who had grown up in Babylonia. Those who remained behind and did not participate in the return continued to be Jews, with synagogues, scriptures, and other characteristic features of Jewish life. The famous passage in Acts 2:5-11 gives some idea of the dispersion of Jews throughout the Mediterranean and the Middle East. As a result of this situation it could be said that in the middle of the first Christian century there were two centers of Jewish life and thought—Jerusalem and Alexandria.

163 What about Jerusalem?

The religious center of all Judaism was the Jerusalem Temple, up until the time of the destruction of the city at the hands of the Roman general Titus in A.D. 70. To it every Jew in the world was supposed to make certain pilgrimages, and toward its support every Jew was expected to make an annual contribution. So important was the latter that certain designated officials in Alexandria, in Egypt, gave all their time to the task of collecting and forwarding the funds. To the sacred altar in the Holy City the hearts of all the Jews turned in a devotion and loyalty that is one of the most remarkable facts in all the life of the East. Schools of theology, presided over by world famous Jewish scholars, were conducted under the shadow of the Temple; the decrees of the Sanhedrin became binding on Jews thousands of miles removed from the Holy Land; the judgments and opinions of the Jerusalem doctors of the law carried great weight everywhere in Jewry.

164 What about Alexandria?

Alexander the Great, in conquering the world, found the Jews valuable friends, and to them he showed numerous favors. When he founded the magnificent city of Alexandria in Egypt, he encouraged the Jews to settle therein by various devices and special benefits, with the result that in Jesus' day the Jewish population of Alexandria was greater than the total population of Jerusalem. The Alexandrian Jews were Greek-speaking, for the most part, and under the influence of Greek learning and culture they had built up one of the great universities of the world. In scholarship and in general learning they were Greek, and in many respects they were much more liberal and advanced than their coreligionists in Jerusalem. They were the ones, as has been described (Question 50), who translated the Hebrew scriptures into the Greek version known as the Septuagint, which was used by Greek-speaking Jews and Christians everywhere throughout the Roman world.

165 Did they all agree on the Old Testament?

There was almost universal agreement among the Jews of all sections of the world concerning the books making up the two divisions of scripture known as the Law and the Prophets. There might be a bit more confidence in the Law, as an inspired writing, than in the Prophets. In Jerusalem, for example, the Sadducees had raised some doubts about the Prophets, although the popular esteem in which they were held admitted of very little question concerning their inspiration. In the main, however, relatively few distinctions were drawn between Isaiah, for example, and Moses. Such debate as there was centered about the authority the books in the third division, called the Writings.

166 What is the Law?

The first five books of the Old Testament (frequently referred to by Christians as the Pentateuch) formed a single continuous work credited to Moses and known to the Jews as the Book of the Torah (Law). This monumental work was actually a compilation put together in its present form by Jewish scholars, prophets, priests, and leaders during the period of the Exile. Then, brought back to Jerusalem about the year 400 B.C., it served in something of the capacity of a constitution for the restored Israel. Containing as it did the original ten "words," or "commandments" of Moses, together with a multitude of interpretations and applications thereof, the Torah contained the heart and core of the nation's faith, and the basis of its civil and ecclesiastical government. In Jesus' day the Jews believed that they knew the will of God for mankind, and that it was contained in the Torah and interpreted by their own legalistic codes and ceremonies.

167 What are the Prophets?

Beginning with a shepherd named Amos, about 750 B.C., and continuing for several hundred years, great religious thinkers and preachers had appeared among the Hebrews, voicing profound social, economic, political, and religious opinions concerning the life of the people and the government of the nation, and passing on their sermons in written form. Because the people believed that the prophets "spoke for God," their teachings carried great weight, especially when they were written down and conserved. In time there grew up a prophetic party which interpreted history according to prophetic principles, thus producing the books (Joshua, Judges, Samuel, Kings) known as the "Former Prophets," the works of the prophets themselves (Isaiah, Jeremiah, Ezekiel, and "The Twelve") being known as the "Latter Prophets."

168 What are the Writings?

A collection of books of varying degrees of spiritual value which, for one good reason or another, had won a status among the people as a result of which they were accorded great respect. Opinion was divided concerning their inspiration, and in Jesus' day they ranked lower than the Law and the Prophets. However, there are in the Gospels several references to the Psalms which show that at least this one book of the Writings was looked upon as scripture. The primary point of debate was just which other books should be accepted as having the same status and which should be considered not inspired. Since the question was not finally decided until after Christianity was separated from Judaism, the Jews and Christians did not reach exactly the same decision. This fact gave rise to the problem of the books called Apocrypha, about which there is a difference of opinion to this day.

169 What are the Apocrypha?

As it happened among the Christians in the case of the New Testament and other religious writings, so it happened among the Jews that a considerable body of religious literature grew up—some of it of high spiritual value—which never quite achieved the rank of scripture. The name "Apocrypha" came to be given to a group of fourteen such which were held in such high esteem by the Alexandrian Jews that they were included in the Greek Old Testament (the Septuagint), but which were rejected by the Jews generally and never became a part of the Hebrew Bible.

170 What are the names of the Apocryphal books?

First and Second Esdras, Tobit, Judith, the Additions to the book of Esther, the Wisdom of Solomon, the Wisdom of Jesus Son of Sirach (Ecclesiasticus), Baruch, the Epistle of Jeremy, the Additions to the Book of Daniel, the Prayer of Manasses, and First and Second Maccabees.

171 Who wrote the Apocrypha?

Just as in the case of the writings in the Old Testament, the Apocrypha were written by devout and patriotic Jews. Each had a religious theme, and each was written to serve a spiritual purpose. But because they could not qualify as scripture according to a specification laid down by certain other Jews, they never attained the rank of "inspired" works.

172 What was that specification?

Those Jews who looked to Jerusalem for their spiritual authority had the idea that all inspiration ceased with Ezra and Nehemiah, about 400 B.C. Accordingly their rigid requirement for any work of scripture was age—it must be over four centuries old. Others, notably the Alexandrian scholars, believed that God continued to speak to godly men as the occasion required, regardless of the time element. It was natural, therefore, for the Alexandrian Jews to believe various books were inspired which the Palestinian Jews could not accept. As a matter of fact, however, it turned out that the Palestinian Jews did accept certain books written after the time of Ezra because their means for judging the dates of writings were untrustworthy.

173 How did they judge the dates?

It must be remembered that few ancient Jewish writers had

any reason to sign their names to their work. Of the books about which there was doubt in the first century, only one bore the name of the actual author—the Wisdom of Jesus Son of Sirach, better known today by the title Ecclesiasticus. Because this Jesus was known to have lived early in the second century B.C., his work was obviously written too late to be "inspired"—this in spite of its high literary and spiritual value and its widespread popularity. Similarly, the books of Maccabees were obviously late because they dealt with historical events of the second century. Certain other books could easily be recognized as late because they existed only in Greek—a language known to have been first brought to the Middle East by Alexander the Great nearly a century after Ezra's time. For the rest, however, the first-century Jews seem to have had no way of telling the dates of the books, with the result that they accepted at least two—Daniel and Esther—which scholars today can definitely date later than the time of Jesus Son of Sirach.

174 When was the matter settled?

As long as the Temple stood in Jerusalem, and the high priest sat upon his throne, Judaism had a center to which it could turn and an authority which could settle disputes. But with the destruction of Jerusalem in A.D. 70, and the scattering of the Palestinian Jews, a serious need was felt for some center around which the faith could be gathered. Quite naturally the Jewish leaders turned their minds toward their scriptures. After the emperor's edict that Jerusalem should not be rebuilt, a new Jewish city named Jamnia began to grow up about thirty miles from the site of Jerusalem, in the direction of the sea. To this new metropolis an impressive body of learned men gathered, and in time a highly reputable university came into existence. Sometime about A.D. 90 a more or less representative gathering of influential Jews came together here for the purpose of discussing various matters of interest to the Jewish people, and among the issues discussed was the question of the scriptures. Oddly enough, the Christians seem to have contributed to that result.

175 How did the Christians contribute?

Some of the Christian Gospels were in circulation by this time and evidently were proving very attractive to devout Jewish readers. The Christians were beginning to make some claims about their inspiration, and the Jews may have felt it necessary to define their scriptures more precisely.

176 Did they come to agreement at Jamnia?

In one sense they did—on the subject of the books making up the Hebrew text of the Law, the Prophets, and the Writings. In another they did not. The Alexandrian Jews continued to use their Greek scriptures containing the Apocrypha, and it was some time before all the dispersion Jews accepted the Hebrew canon. Interestingly enough, the dispute carried on out into the Christian ranks and remains to plague us in a measure even to this day.

177 How did the dispute get into the Christian world?

It must be remembered that the Old Testament of the early Christians was the Greek translation, the Septuagint, which consisted of the books selected by the Alexandrian Jews. Thus most Christians took the Apocrypha for granted as a part of the Old Testament, not even realizing that they were in any way different from the rest, and most of the early Christian writers quote them often as scripture.

178 Did the Apocrypha remain in the Christian Old Testament?

After a time the more scholarly among Christian leaders discovered that these writings were not in the Hebrew text and began to question their canonicity. But by then they were so well established in usage that few people were worried by doubts about them. When Jerome was preparing his Vulgate, he consulted the Hebrew text and followed it as much as he dared. He personally believed the Hebrew text to contain the only inspired Old Testament scriptures, and he referred to the books not found in it as Apocrypha (literally "hidden"). But these books were so thoroughly established that Jerome felt he must include them in his version. Thus the Apocrypha passed over into the Vulgate, which became the official text of the Roman Catholic Church. Meanwhile the eastern half of the church continued to use the Septuagint itself, so that the Apocrypha remained in the Old Testament of the Greek

Orthodox Church also. Thus the Apocrypha remained in the Old Testaments of two of the great branches of the Christian Church.

179 Are the Apocrypha in the Protestant Old Testament?

They are not a part of the Old Testament in Protestant Bibles. When printed at all, they are gathered together in a separate section labeled "Apocrypha" (instead of being scattered through the Old Testament without distinction as in the Roman and Greek Bibles), so that the reader can recognize that they are on a different plane from the other books.

180 How did they come to be separated?

Martin Luther, the great German reformer who launched the Protestant movement, based his arguments and actions on the Bible, which he studied exhaustively. From his researches into the Scriptures in the original languages, and into ancient and contemporary commentaries on them, he became convinced that these writings which he did not find in the Hebrew were not inspired scripture that could be relied on in doctrinal matters. Accordingly, in publishing his translation of the Bible into German, he set them off in an appendix to the Old Testament, with the title suggested by Jerome, "Apocrypha." In an explanatory note he stated that these books were "useful and good for reading" but were "not held equal to the sacred Scriptures." In this view we may suspect that Luther was somewhat influenced by the relation of some of the Apocrypha to certain Protestant doctrines he was preaching.

181 How did the Apocrypha affect Protestant doctrines?

Martin Luther was a very independent as well as penetrating thinker. He based his Protestant principles on the teachings of Jesus and Paul, believing these to be the essence of the Scriptures. When he came across something that seemed to favor a different viewpoint, he did not see how it could belong in the Bible. He would have been happy, for example, to have eliminated the Epistle of James from the New Testament. He called it a "right strawy epistle," because it did not support the

Protestant doctrine of justification by faith but rather seemed to demand good works, which Luther's Romanist opponents could claim as support for indulgences and such. Luther could not find any basis for expunging James from his New Testament; but when he discovered several passages in the Apocrypha being quoted in defense of the priestly requirements of penance and good works, there was something he could do. The ancient Jews had refused to admit the Apocrypha to the Hebrew Bible, and this fact furnished the doughty monk the precedent he needed for pushing them out of the German Bible.

182 Did other Protestants follow his lead?

The other early reformers agreed with Luther and even went beyond him in belittling the Apocrypha. Of most interest to us is the fact that Miles Coverdale conferred with Luther and adopted the same treatment for his own translation, which appeared as the first complete printed English Bible just the year after Luther's complete German Bible was published. Thus the precedent of placing the Apocrypha in an appendix was begun, and was followed in practically all English Protestant Bibles until they came to be omitted entirely.

183 When were the Apocrypha dropped from Protestant Bibles?

The Thirty-nine Articles, the series of statements by which the Church of England declared its faith after separating from Rome, recommended the Apocrypha "for example of life and instruction of manners," even though not "to establish any doctrine." But Puritan sentiment tended toward a definite distaste for the Apocrypha, and in 1629 this resulted in a radical innovation—an edition of the Bible (King James Version) with the Apocrypha left out entirely. The omission stirred much criticism at the time, but other such editions were issued from time to time, until Bibles without the Apocrypha became the more common type. The dropping of the Apocrypha was therefore no sudden action, but rather a gradual shift of public sentiment over many years.

184 What is the status of the case today?

The Thirty-nine Articles are still the creed of the Anglican churches (including the Episcopal Church in the United States as well as the Church of England), and many members of these churches wish to read the Apocrypha today "for example of life and instruction of manners." Many Lutherans also take seriously Martin Luther's similar recommendation. Therefore a few Bible publishers now provide editions of the King James Version containing the Apocrypha. They are also available in the English Revised Version (though not in the American Standard and Revised Standard Versions) and in Dr. Goodspeed's "American Translation." However, no Protestant sect of any numerical importance accepts them as being scripture.

185 What attitude does the Roman Catholic Church take?

The position of the Roman Catholic Church was actually settled for all practical purposes with the publication of Jerome's Vulgate in A.D. 405, but official action about it did not take place till the Protestant Reformation placed this and other beliefs in doubt and led to the Council of Trent in 1546. That body decreed that the entire collection of books as contained in the Septuagint and the Vulgate should be accepted as scripture. The statement issued at that time is still in force and is very clear: "If any man does not accept as sacred and canonical these books entire, with all their parts, as they have customarily been read in the Catholic Church and are contained in the ancient and common Latin edition . . . , let him be anathema." This means that what Protestants call the Apocrypha are to be accepted by Roman Catholics as having the same inspired authority as anything in the Old or the New Testament. In fact they are not Apocrypha but regular parts of the Old Testament to Roman Catholics, who apply the name Apocrypha to an entirely different group of books—the writings which Protestants usually call the Pseudepigrapha.

186 What are the Pseudepigrapha?

The name means "writings of fictitious authorship"; and it is applied to a number of religious books circulating among the Jews in the first Christian century, especially in Alexandria, which were represented as being written by men of the distant past, such as Moses and the patriarchs. Even in Alexandria they do not seem to have been considered scripture by the Jews, since they were not part of the Greek Old Testament adopted by the early Christians; and none of them were ever accepted as scripture by any major group of Christians. However, they were valued enough to exert an influence on the early Christians. There are a number of allusions to one or another of them in the New Testament, and Jude even quotes a lengthy sentence (verses 14-15) from one called the book of Enoch. Each of them seems to have been recommended for at least personal reading by some Christian leader at one time or another. They are of interest today only to the historian or other specialist, however, and it is enough for most of us to know that these Pseudepigrapha exist and that among Roman Catholics they are the writings designated by the name Apocrypha.

187 How should a Protestant look upon the Apocrypha?

The liberty granted to individual Protestants makes it possible for any man to judge their value and authority for himself, without requiring a church council to settle it for him. Consciously or unconsciously the average Protestant probably ascribes a somewhat higher quality of inspiration to certain books of the Bible than to others—at least in the practical matter of reading them for personal guidance. This is what people have been doing ever since the idea of scripture was first conceived.

188 When did the idea of scripture start?

The date was 621 B.C., and it can be fixed rather definitely because the story is told in considerable detail in II Kings 22-23. Before this time the word of God was assumed to be expressed in the spoken statements of inspired prophets about any specific problem at issue. But from this time on it was recognized that God's word enshrined in written form might have a living authority for all sorts of situations of human life. The story of how this revolutionary shift from dependence on prophets to dependence on scripture came about is one of the most interesting and significant in the Old Testament.

189 What is that story?

As has been said, the event occurred in 621 B.C.; and King Josiah, the ruler of the kingdom of Judah at that time, was a leading character in it. However, to understand it clearly we must go back some eighty years earlier, to the closing years of the ministry of the great prophet Isaiah, at the very beginning of the seventh century B.C.

190 What was Isaiah's part in it?

Isaiah was the trusted adviser of King Hezekiah, who was an able and godly ruler, but even with the prophet's wise counsel could hardly cope with the ruthless Assyrian aggression of his day. The tiny kingdom of Judah was repeatedly overrun, and many influential persons in the court attributed the woes of the time to the king's reliance on Isaiah. Becoming discouraged over the attitude of this growing number who were abandoning the worship of Jehovah and calling for alliances that involved pagan worship, Isaiah organized a small group of disciples into a "school of the prophets." To these devoted followers he committed his teachings in the hope that they could somehow stem the tide of ungodliness via public opinion. He looked to them to conserve the national faith in Jehovah regardless of what might happen to him personally when Hezekiah's protection should end.

191 What did happen to Isaiah?

When King Hezekiah died in 696 B.C., his twelve-year-old son Manasseh was placed on the throne, and Isaiah's enemies became the power behind the throne. The Bible does not record what they did to the great prophet, but according to a legend alluded to in Hebrews 11:37 (and told in detail in a book called the Martyrdom of Isaiah, one of the Pseudepigrapha) he was executed by being sawed in two. No doubt this happened while Manasseh was still a boy, but the young king grew up to follow and even outrun his guardians as an implacable foe of the prophetic party. The authors of Kings considered him as the arch villain among all the rulers of Judah, saying that he "shed very much innocent blood, till he had filled Jerusalem from one end to another."

192 What happened to Isaiah's disciples?

Part of them undoubtedly supplied some of the "innocent blood" which Manasseh shed. The rest seem to have been driven underground, where they continued to work together throughout his long reign of fifty-five years, carrying on what activities they could. As so often in the story of Hebrew and Christian faith, persecution served to stimulate zeal that might otherwise have died out.

193 Of what did their activities consist?

They worked along two lines: (1) They kept the national hope alive and cultivated a sentiment among the people which would be fallow soil for a revival of Jehovahism when a new king came to the throne or a favorable opportunity appeared. (2) In anticipation of this new day they seem to have met in secret for the purpose of encouraging one another, strengthening one another's faith, and studying the changing situation. Thus they worked out a legal code which they expected would be adopted by the people when the day came.

194 Did they write a new system of law?

Not exactly. Instead, they studied the ancient laws of Moses, together with such interpretations and applications as had developed through the years, and rewrote them so as to make them apply to the new conditions they confidently expected would exist when the restoration came.

195 What rewriting was needed?

According to the records of the nation Moses had received two tablets of the Law directly from Jehovah on Mount Sinai (Exodus 34:1), but this was an extremely simple code which had to be interpreted as it was applied. Moses himself had found it necessary to amplify the Ten Commandments, in order to make them fit the circumstances of actual life. For example, one of the original commandments forbade labor on the Sabbath day, but someone had to define what was, and what was not, labor. In an almost endless variety of ways the original laws had to be elaborated to meet the changing conditions, as is illustrated in the case of the rule which forbade coveting.

196 What about the law concerning coveting?

There are at least two versions of the Ten Commandments in our Old Testaments (Exodus 20:3-17 and Deuteronomy 5:7-21). In one of them the Hebrew is commanded not to covet his neighbor's house (Exodus 20:17) and in the other (Deuteronomy 5:21) he is also forbidden to covet his neighbor's field. Some historians believe the first was written to apply to the life of the people in the wilderness, before any man owned any land, and that the second is an elaboration made necessary when the nation invaded Palestine and became landowners. In several ways the two Decalogues show slight differences, which can usually be explained on the basis of a changed pattern of life among the people.

197 What did the prophets hope to accomplish?

They believed the wicked and godless governments would be displaced with a government loyal to Jehovah, and they wanted to be ready for that day with a legal code which would establish the ancient Jehovahism.

198 How did they proceed?

They prepared their system of law, probably at the cost of infinite pains and endless discussion, and formulated it in precise language. All this they wrote in a book, saving the volume for an auspicious occasion when, the conditions being considered favorable, they might bring it out and secure its acceptance by a friendly government.

199 What did they do with the book?

They probably kept it secreted in some hiding place known only to the members of their own group, until the day came when a friendly king might sit upon the throne.

200 Did such a king come to the throne?

Manasseh's grandson, the young King Josiah, came to the throne in the year 639 B.C. He was only eight years old at the time, but as he matured he began to exhibit a godly interest in the ancient faith of the nation—so much so that in the year 621 he ordered a rehabilitation of the Temple, which had fallen into a sad state of repair during Manasseh's reign. In the belief that he might be the man who would restore the ancient faith, the prophets hid their book in the Temple where they knew that it would be discovered and laid before the king.

201 What happened?

The workers came upon the book and, sensing that it was of great importance, turned it over to Hilkiah, the high priest. He in turn put it into the hands of Shaphan, the king's secretary, who immediately presented it to the king himself. No one seemed to know precisely what the book was, or what should be done with it, though all agreed that it was extremely important and must be treated reverently. At that point a woman entered the story.

202 Who was the woman?

A prophetess named Huldah, the wife of the officer in charge of the royal wardrobe. Many scholars believe she may have been a member of the prophetic party, secretly. At any rate she seems to have had the confidence of the king and also knew something about the history and purpose of the book. Upon examining it carefully (and it is easy to imagine the scene), she warned King Josiah that the strange writing was the Book of the Law of Jehovah, and that if he would order the affairs of his kingdom in accordance with its principles, all would be well. God would bless the nation, and him. If not, ruin awaited them all.

203 Was the king impressed?

Upon the occasion when he first saw the book he exhibited great concern, but Huldah's report was even more convincing—so much so that a great convocation of the nation was held at which the Book of the Law was read to the assembled multitude and declared to be the new code for the nation (II Kings 23:1-27). Then ensued a great popular demonstration, new vows of loyalty to Jehovah were registered, and a general cleanup of the national life followed.

204 What did this mean?

It meant that from this time on the Hebrews were "a people of a book." The highest law of their land was not the whimsical decree of a king, but the law of God contained in a book which anyone might read. In other words, the people now had something like a written constitution.

205 What laws did the book contain?

Comparing the account of the measure King Josiah took in his reform with the groups of laws found in the Pentateuch shows that discovery of those found in the book of Deuteronomy would be most likely to produce the results described in Second Kings. Therefore the scholars practically all agree that the Book of the Law which Shaphan delivered to King Josiah was substantially what we find now in chapters 5-26 and 28 of this book. In doing so they are identifying the main portion of the book of Deuteronomy as the foundation on which the entire Bible was built.

206 How is this true?

This original Book of the Law was the first literary material produced by the Hebrews which can be said to have achieved the rank of scripture. It is thus the core about which developed not only the great Book of the Law that is now the first section of the Hebrew Bible, but in fact the entire Bible, both Old and New Testaments—for the whole idea of sacred scripture started here. It is interesting that it was a woman who first proclaimed it.

207 How was further material added?

To continue the story we must move on about a generation later to the year 586 B.C., when the city of Jerusalem fell to the Babylonians after a three-year siege. The proud capital was completely destroyed—Temple, royal palace, public buildings, private residences, and the surrounding walls. Here we come to one of the most dramatic scenes in all Hebrew history.

208 What was the nature of that scene?

With the walls of the city breached, and the Temple laid waste, the battered and wounded defenders were herded together in a valley below the ancient fortifications and ordered to prepare for the terrible trek across the desert to Babylonia. The exhausting trip had to be made on foot, with practically no animals to carry their goods for them. The desert was barren, desolate, and forbidding, and the nights could be bitterly cold. A poor wretch who happened to be without a great cloak could almost be certain of suffering. As the captives were herded together preparatory to making the terrible trek, here and there among them were to be seen heroic souls who, determined to save the sacred treasures of their faith, were carrying the large rolls in their baggage whereon were written the sermons of the prophets, the ancient history of the nation, and other precious documents. In some cases it was no doubt necessary for the burdened people to choose between the rolls and their great cloaks, and many must have chosen to suffer from the cold rather than leave the rolls behind. Everything we have in the Bible which goes back of the destruction of Jerusalem in 586 B.C. is based on these rolls saved by brave and devout Hebrews who, even as they trudged wearily across the desert to their exile in Babylonia, were beginning to ponder the most baffling religious problem the nation had ever faced.

209 What was that baffling problem?

On that awful day when the walls of the Holy City were breached by the Babylonians the adventure begun at Sinai seemingly came to an end. Now all the best citizens of Judah were being carried off to captivity. Their whole religious system was destroyed, and the covenant with Jehovah seemed to have become meaningless. Earlier the little northern kingdom of Israel had come to a similar disastrous end at the hands of the Assyrians in 721 B.C., and now the last of the chosen race had fallen. The question the leaders had to face, then, was a very simple one: What had been the cause of the nation's disaster and failure? Was Jehovah unable to fulfill his promise to guide and protect his chosen people? Had he been overcome by the gods of the Babylonians? Why had the agreement reached at Sinai come to such an inglorious end?

210 What was the answer to the question?

There seemed to be but two possible answers: either God had failed the people or the people had failed God. There were those, of course, who accepted the first. In the belief that the Babylonian gods had conquered they went over to that worship. They were evidently no more than a small number, but there were at least some. On the other hand, those who believed that the people had failed God were scarcely settled in Babylonia before they went at the task of discovering how this could have happened and, more important, how it could be prevented from happening again. In this they had the help of some great souls—prophets, scribes, priests, and learned men of the law. These set about to study the case from the beginning.

211 What did they have to study?

They had the rolls which they had carried across the desert at such sacrifice—the rolls containing the literature and the history of the nation. These furnished both the declaration of Jehovah's expectations of his people and the record of their shortcomings.

212 What did they discover?

As these leaders studied the great mass of manuscripts they had brought over into the Exile with them, they found first of all the confirmation that their troubles were a direct result of their failure to live up to God's demands. The written sermons of Amos, Hosea, Micah, Isaiah, and the rest of the prophets were full of warnings that the sins of the nation would result in just such disaster as had overtaken them.

213 What hope did they see for the future?

However dark the present situation, as well as the example of the sister kingdom of Israel a century and a half earlier, the people of Judah could not believe that Jehovah had cast them off entirely. Rather they persisted in the faith that someday they would be permitted to return to the Promised Land and re-establish their nation. For this belief they discovered some foundation in certain promises the prophet Jeremiah had written just before the great catastrophe. Moreover, after many years in Babylon there arose among the exiles themselves a new prophet who made even more definite promises of redemption for God's people. His name has not come down to us, but he is generally referred to as Second Isaiah because his poems came to be added to the book of Isaiah (beginning with chapter 40) and have been preserved for us there. Having this hope of restoration, therefore, they set to work to codify their records of Jehovah's will for them, that they might have a detailed guide to serve as their constitution, their religious philosophy, and their civil law. Thus they produced a new and enlarged Book of the Law.

214   How did this differ from the earlier book?

The Book of the Law accepted as the first work of scripture in King Josiah's day took its place as one of the key portions of the enlarged book, but to it were added a number of other documents. These included other law codes and also historical accounts of their presumed origin in the earliest beginnings of the nation, especially the days of the great lawgiver, Moses. All these were combined into one great work so long that five papyrus rolls were needed for it. It was this enlarged Book of the Law that Ezra the scribe brought with him to Jerusalem in 397 B.C. In doing this he planned a very unusual thing of great historic interest.

215   What was that historic thing?

Ezra's purpose in making the trip to Judah was to lead in the restoration of the Temple and the nation. He had full authority to do so from the Persian government. But he also had the Book of the Law, which he proposed should become the foundation of the new state. It was rooted deep in the teachings and principles of Moses, the founder of the nation. The people were ill prepared for a great spiritual adventure, however, for the years during which the Hebrew government had been broken and crushed had taken a heavy toll. To summon them to true dignity and to inspire them to heroic effort, Ezra planned something very spectacular. The Book of the Law must be adopted as the official code in a great meeting of the entire nation, democratically planned. The acceptance of the book must represent a popular tide of approval, and not a mere submission to authority.

216   How did Ezra proceed?

Without divulging all of his secret, Ezra let it be known that he had brought with him from Babylon a message of vast importance. By playing skillfully upon the curiosity of the people through a period of days he aroused great expectancy. Then one morning, after due announcement, he took up his position before the Water Gate (Nehemiah 8:1). Flanked on either side by certain leaders of the people, he began to read. As he read one phrase or sentence, the leaders would repeat it, shouting the words so that all could hear. From time to time

Levites took time out to explain to the people exactly what the legislation meant. For three days this went on until the entire book (all of Genesis, Exodus, Leviticus, Numbers, Deuteronomy) had been read and explained. Then in a great popular vote the people agreed to accept it as binding upon them and their children forever. It was the most democratic religious episode in all human history up to that time (Nehemiah 8—10).

217 What significance did this have for the scripture?

It meant that the great Book of the Law, based on the ancient code of Moses, elaborated and interpreted by the school of the prophets which Isaiah had founded, and compiled with such meticulous care by the great scholars of the Exile, was selected to be the scripture, the constitution, and the rock base of the people's government. It was voted by the multitude, every citizen being allowed to participate. Nothing like it had ever occurred before. Therefore our Pentateuch, which has come down to us as the hard core of the Old Testament, was selected and voted to be scripture by the people themselves.

218 Did the people know they were voting for the scriptures?

The word "scripture" had not yet come into use among the Jews, and no such concept as our modern idea of a divinely inspired Bible was known among them. But they did vote to accept the great Book of the Law as being the law of God, binding upon their nation and upon them as individuals. It was, to them, the final authority. Their respect for it depended, not upon the fact that it was authored by men of great wisdom, but upon the fact that it had been authorized by God. The divine authority with which it was invested gave it its effectiveness in the government of the life of the nation.

219 How did the other books become attached?

Once the idea of certain divinely inspired writings as the source of knowledge of God's will became established, it was natural that other writings of similar character and similar spiritual helpfulness should impress men as belonging to the same class. Thus the prophetic literature kept growing in status. In their own day the prophets had enjoyed great power as a result of the fact that the people believed they were spokesmen for God. With their passing the written sermons they left behind them inherited much of this respect. In time the people came to believe these scrolls to have been inspired in much the same way as the Law. There never was any formal action in the matter. Instead, it seems to have been a popular judgment which emerged with the years. All we can discover about it is that by about 200 B.C. the books of the Former Prophets and the Latter Prophets were viewed as scripture. In something of the same fashion the Writings later came to be associated with the Law and the Prophets, and in Jesus' day were in the process of being accepted as scripture. Public opinion, developing through long periods of use, settled the matter, the final decision at Jamnia about A.D. 90 being simply a ratification of established custom. As we have seen, the selection of the New Testament canon followed a similar pattern. All this seems to have at least some bearing on an important point.

220 What is that point?

That the inspiration of the Bible is best proved by its power to inspire. It is this power to inspire which formed the actual basis for the judgments of both Jews and Christians when they were allowed free choices in selecting the books that make up our Bible. The formal councils, such as the one held at Jamnia, only gave official expression to the canon already chosen by the people over years of use. In this connection it should be recognized that even today the individual Christian has a voice in determining the canon of scripture for the present and the future.

221 How can the individual today affect the canon?

We think of the canon today as having been fixed long ago; yet for all practical purposes the canon is not what some denominational rule declares, but rather what people read and order their lives by. In this respect it is not so fixed as might appear at first glance. The Apocrypha offer a good example. Some Protestants wish them included in their Bibles, but most do not. The Bible publishers print the respective editions according to popular demand, with most omitting the Apocrypha; but a change in public sentiment about this would quickly be reflected in the publishers' offerings. On the other hand various abridged editions of the Bible are constantly being placed on the market. If such a shortened Bible should appeal to Christians so much that multitudes of them would use it in place of the complete Bible, then the canon would be effectively reduced thereby, even though the change might not be officially recognized. This leads us to an important final thought about the canon.

222 What is that final thought?

That each Bible reader creates his or her own canon of scripture. The reader judges the Bible in the light created from experience. Many long passages are of little spiritual value to us, and others are of the greatest value. Most of us turn to a relatively small portion of the Scriptures for our inspiration and guidance. As we learn more about other portions, we were able to understand and be inspired by much that was meaningless before. Accordingly it might perhaps be said that the primary purpose of the following studies in this series is to help the reader add new books to his or her practical working canon.